SEND ME THE FLOWERS
BEFORE
YOU DIE

A Guide to Lessening the Burdens for
Those You Leave Behind

Marie C, Robinson

ISBN-10:1517036534
ISBN-13:978-1517036539

DEDICATION

To my husband Darrol, our children Christine and Steven and our grandson Zachary, I love you with all my being.
To my mother, Gabrielle C. Carrier, I am eternally grateful for your love and trust and showing me how to give of myself.

ACKNOWLEDGMENTS

I would like to thank all of you who have touched my life. There are too many to list here. I will always be grateful for your encouragement, counsel and friendship and for having a belief in my vision to help others one at a time.

Thank you Darrol Robinson, Christine & Bob Paquette, Steven & Jessica & Zachary Robinson, Gerry & Suzanne Carrier, Jana McLain and John Galbreath for keeping me accountable and encouraging me to get this book done.

Thank you Patricia Rainboth, Director and founder of Victims, Inc., for teaching me the tools to help others. Patrick Snow, thank you for getting me on the right path to writing this book. Tom Corson Knowles, thank you for giving me the tools to publish this book. A special thank you to Wendy Lipton-Dibner for helping me to make my impact.

Introduction

"Send Me the Flowers Before You Die". A guide to lessening the burden for those you leave behind. Learn how your wishes can be carried out when you die and beyond.

This book will help you prepare for the end of your life and make it a lot easier for your loved ones to deal with your death.

Stories will demonstrate to you the real day-to-day messes left behind for your loved ones and what you can do to prevent this from happening to your family.

This book will show you how you can make your own decisions for the end of your life and beyond, leaving your loved ones with written instructions on what your wishes are. Legally, no one can change what you want done.

The burden of making life decisions by your loved ones will be lifted and they will not have the guilt that comes with making a life ending or sustaining decision. They will forever ask the question, "Did I do the right thing?"

By being prepared, you are enabling your loved ones to grieve for you without a lot of additional time, expense and emotional stress to close out your estate.

You can be in control even after you die.

Let me show you how!

CONTENTS

1: No Will

"Where there's a will, there's a way."

Proverb

You Choose

I would like to tell you a story about a woman named Rose.

Rose is an older woman who was widowed five years ago. Rose lived on the West Coast and was quite active. She was quite healthy for her age. She never had any children. She had a cousin that she stayed in touch with, who lived on the East Coast. Her name was Trish and Rose was her only living relative.

Rose and her cousin Trish spoke on the phone every week. They had been doing this for many years when one day Rose received a phone call from the police department from the town that her cousin lived in. The police told Rose that her cousin Trish was found dead in her home. A neighbor, checking on her, found her on the floor unresponsive and cold. The neighbor had immediately called 911. The Medical Examiner determined that Trish had a heart attack and died. Rose was very sorry for the loss of her cousin. She surely would miss her.

Police got in touch with Rose because her name and phone number were beside the phone. The police asked Rose to come to the East Coast to handle her cousins' arrangements.

Rose arranged to fly to the East Coast, some 2500 miles away. She planned to stay on the East Coast for several weeks. Rose arranged, for her animals care, her mail to be forwarded to the East Coast and she cancelled her personal appointments. On the plane, Rose started thinking about what Trish had left (or not left) behind. She did not know if Trish would want cremation, a funeral, or to be buried. Did she have a burial plot? Did she have a Will? They never spoke of any of these things. Rose really had no idea what to expect.

When she arrived at the home of her cousin, a neighbor was there to greet her. The neighbor told her the name of the funeral home that the police had called. After freshening up a bit, she called the funeral director and made an appointment to see him.

Rose scoured the house for any paperwork that Trish may have had that would help her. She found some bills and bank statements but not much else, until she looked under the bed and found a fireproof safe. The safe was not locked and she found a birth certificate, the house deed, and a life insurance policy. There was no Will in the safe. She looked in Trish's purse and found a checkbook and a savings passbook.

Rose met with the funeral director. After some discussion with him, she decided that cremation was the best solution. Rose was not aware of Trish having any church affiliations or a cemetery plot. Before cremation took place, Rose had to get a death certificate. Unfortunately, Rose did not have the information needed to get the death certificate so she decided to hire an attorney.

The attorney was willing to go through public records and find out Trish's parents full names, where they were born, their dates of birth, their dates of death and where they died. After the attorney gathered the information needed, Rose was able to get a death certificate and have her cousin cremated. After a few weeks, the funeral director gave Rose Trish's ashes.

Because Trish had not left a will, it would be up to a Probate Judge to designate someone to oversee Trish's estate. Rose had no experience in dealing with the Probate Court. She was a teenager when her father died and her mother inherited everything automatically. When her mother died from cancer in a nursing home, there was nothing left for Rose. All of her mother's assets had been depleted for her care.

The attorney made a list of all of Trish's assets and filed all the necessary forms to the Probate Court. Since Rose was the only living relative, the judge named her as the executor and beneficiary of Trish's estate. All the assets that Trish had, including cash, were frozen (could not be used) until her estate was Probated. When the process was complete, Rose had the power to manage Trish's estate with the oversight of the court and the help of the attorney.

Rose was the beneficiary on the life insurance policy and was able to claim $10,000 without going through the court.

Anything jointly owned or with a designated named beneficiary does not have to go through Probate.

The Probate process took several months and was very expensive. As executor, Rose had many things to do.

Rose had to:

Pay all the outstanding bills.

Close the checking and savings account.

Clear out and sell the house.

Cancel all utilities.

Sell the car.

Inform the Social Security Administration and other interested parties of Trish's death.

The Social Security Administration had sent Trish's monthly check. The check was sent back to the Government.

Eventually everything was complete and Rose received the proceeds from the remainder of the estate.

Rose finally got a chance to relax a little bit. She got to thinking about how much easier this would have been had her cousin prepared for her demise. She was a little upset that she had to go through so much to get her cousins estate closed out. This was an expensive and enormous task. If only Trish had written everything down on paper, the Probate process would have been faster, easier and less expensive.

Rose decided she would not leave this type of mess for her niece Amanda, who would inherit her estate.

Rose called an attorney to have a Will made. She included an Advanced Directive that told Amanda that she did not want to be on life support or have any measures taken to keep her alive if something happened to her; she wanted comfort care only. A Durable Power of Attorney document was drawn-up for financial decisions. This would allow Amanda to take control of her aunt's medical decisions and manage her money if Rose could not make those decisions herself.

Rose also prepaid her funeral. She copied all these documents and sent them to Amanda. This would make it so much easier for her niece to know what Rose wanted and allow her niece not to have to make any decisions and to begin the healing process sooner after Rose died.

Trish should have done the following to make things easier and less expensive:

- Left a large envelope, with all the necessary documents and titles in one place and made sure Rose knew where it was located.

- Left a Will naming Rose or someone else as the executor of her will and named Rose as the beneficiary.

- Been specific about how she wanted her remains to be disposed of.

- All of this would have made the process more efficient and would have caused Rose far less stress and frustration.

- What can you do to prevent this situation? What do you need to prepare so your loved ones will not have to face the same burden as Rose?

- Create a binder, folder or large envelope with the following documentation:

- Last Will and Testament, a Will is a necessity whether you own any assets or not.

- A Will directs the Probate Court to do what you desire in an organized way including how you want your remains taken care of as well as how to dispose of all your personal items.

- Your parent's full names including mother's maiden name.

- A Birth Certificate

- A Deed to the Property

- A Title to the vehicle

- A list of bank accounts

- Insurance policy

- Other important documents

Tragic Results

This is a story about John and Roberta, a young couple with two children, looking forward to the future.

John was a young man when he died suddenly. He was only 30 years old. John had been living with his girlfriend Roberta for the last seven years. They had two children together under the age of seven. Mike was five years old and Marion was three years old.

One morning when John did not get up at his usual time, Roberta sent Mike in to wake up his daddy. Mike tried very hard to wake his daddy; he shook him and tried to open his eyes. When Mike came back into the kitchen, he was crying and said, "He could not wake up daddy". Roberta ran into the bedroom and found John unresponsive but still warm. She checked to see if she could feel a pulse. She could not. She called 911.

The police and paramedics arrived and they tried to revive John by doing CPR compressions. They shocked his heart to no avail. John was dead. The police called the Medical Examiner to determine the circumstances of John's death. The Medical examiner arrived and examined John. He looked around for any prescriptions and spoke to Roberta about John. Because there was no obvious cause of death, John would have to undergo an autopsy. The Medical Examiner arranged for the transport of John's body to the State capital for an autopsy by the State Forensic Pathologist.

The police notified John's parents of his death. John's parents lived in another state and it took them two and a half hours to arrive at the house.

Roberta was so emotionally upset and unbelieving that it was very hard for her to break this news to her children. The children were crying and she had to attempt to tell her children that their father was dead.

Roberta took the children aside and tried to explain to them that their daddy was dead. His body did not work anymore and that it was broken and could not be fixed. She told them that his body was going to be leaving the house and the doctor would find out what happened to their daddy. She told them they could still talk to him and he would hear them but he could not answer them. His spirit went up to Heaven. She tried to make sure that they knew it was not their fault or anyone's fault that daddy had died. She said that God needed daddy more than they did and that he would be looking down on them and watching over them always. This was the most difficult thing she had ever done.

Meanwhile, John's body was taken to the morgue for autopsy, to determine the cause of death. John and Roberta had been living together for the last seven years but because they were not legally married and he died intestate (without a Will), his parents became the next of kin. That tragically put them in charge of everything including all of his assets, his house, his car, his life insurance, his 401K retirement account and money in the bank.

When John's parents arrived, they were still in shock and had all kinds of questions that Roberta could not answer. Everyone was very upset and could not believe that this happened. They did not stay very long.

John's parents had never been accepting of John and Roberta's relationship. They had never really liked her and therefore, they did not include her in the arrangements for John's funeral. When the State Pathologist called to tell the family his findings of a genetic heart condition that caused John's death, he spoke with John's parents. John was born with a heart defect that went unnoticed from his birth to his death. When John's body was released, it was to his parents. John's parents did not consult or inform Roberta about anything. They made all the funeral arrangements and had their son cremated and buried in a private ceremony that did not include Roberta and her children. John's parents filed all the paperwork for the Probate Court without informing Roberta.

Because John had not arranged for Roberta or their children, they were left in the dark. Roberta, never informed of the autopsy results, was devastated. Roberta found out from a friend that John's father became the Executor of his estate and the beneficiary of John's estate. She did not realize that she could have made an appeal to the court for her children.

John's parents inherited the house and all his assets. They were the beneficiaries of his life insurance and retirement benefits. John never changed the beneficiary on his policies from his parents to Roberta. John's parents sold the house, forcing Roberta and her children to find another place to live. They collected the insurance and retirement benefits and gave nothing to Roberta and her children. Roberta had no family to fall back on for support. Roberta had to move to an apartment with her two children and try to live on her paycheck only. Because John's name was on the birth certificates of both children, Roberta was able to collect from his Social Security benefits for the children. If it had not been for these benefits, it would have been even more devastating for Roberta. John's parents never contacted Roberta or their grandchildren ever again. Roberta was not advised that she could have made an appeal to the court for her children to receive some of the proceeds from John's estate.

Everyone reacts and grieves differently to the death of a loved one, friend or someone they know. Unfortunately, John's parents decided to have nothing to do with Roberta or their grandchildren. Because John did not arrange for Roberta and his children. Roberta and her children, grieved for a very long time, struggled to make ends meet and went through very difficult times.

Planning at any age could have made the situation more manageable for everyone. The loss of anyone we love is devastating enough but with proper planning, it does become a less stressful for those left behind.

Without a Will in place, the court could decide how your assets are distributed. This is a much more expensive process.

If you choose not to marry your significant other, make sure the following documents are in place.

- A last Will and Testament.

- Choose an Executor for your Will, who will insure your wishes are met.

- If you have minor children, be sure to name a guardian for them.

- Choose appropriate beneficiaries for your insurance policies.

- Choose appropriate beneficiaries for your retirement accounts.

Doing the Right Thing

Jim and Frank were in a loving relationship. They were well known in their community where they lived for the last twenty years. One day Frank and Jim left home as usual to go to work. When Frank was not home by six PM, Jim got worried. He turned on the TV to the local news and heard there had been a serious car accident. Pictures at the scene, showed the car involved. He recognized the car as being the same as Frank's. Now he was very worried. He called the police to find out if it was Frank in the accident. The police could not tell him anything. The name of the accident victim was not being released until the notification to the next of kin. Frank and Julie (Frank's sister) lost their parents two years previously. Julie was next of kin.

Julie notified that Frank had been in an accident, was asked to come to the hospital, which she did.

At about 8pm, Julie informed Jim that Frank had died from his injuries in the car accident. Julie had a good relationship with Jim and asked if he would come to the hospital to meet her. Together, Jim and Julie said their last goodbyes to Frank.

Frank did not have a Will. Julie, who was next of kin, handled all the arrangements. Jim was devastated when he realized that Julie had arranged for cremation and not a service. Jim expressed to Julie that Frank's wishes were to be in a crypt.

Unfortunately, Jim did not have any say in what would be done with Frank's remains, since Frank had not put his wishes in writing. Julie understood but found out that cremation was much less expensive. Since her brother had no religious affiliations, she decided that his ashes would be divided between her and Jim. This way Jim would always have Frank with him.

Frank had many assets:

- The home that Frank and Jim lived in.

- A car, (which was totaled in the car accident).

- A retirement plan.

- A life insurance policy.

- Some stock investments.

Various other assets such as tools, furniture, jewelry, etc.

Julie inherited Frank's house. She was also the beneficiary of his retirement plan, insurance policy, and investments. Julie proceeded to file with the Probate Court to become the executor of Frank's estate. Since this was quite straight forward, she did not hire an attorney. Julie, appointed by the court to be the executor of the will, supplied the court with the necessary paperwork to close out the estate. This took many months to accomplish. Jim was living in the house rent free during this time.

When everything was complete, Julie deeded the house to Jim and gave him all of Franks' possessions. Julie kept Frank's investments, life insurance and his retirement accounts.

Jim appreciated what Julie had done for him and thanked her.

Because there was no formal service for Frank, Jim decided to throw a party in his home to celebrate Frank's life. The party was wonderful. All their friends attended and so did Julie.

Jim and Julie are friends but had to butt heads and grieve at the same time, making this a very difficult situation for both of them. They had lost someone they loved and each dealt with that on their own terms.

A will would have enabled Jim and Julie much less frustration and heartache at a time when they were both in a lot of pain.

What can you do to prevent this situation?

- Have a Will stating your wishes for your funeral, end of life celebration, etc.

- Name your partner as executor of your will and allocate to him or her all your possessions.

- Name your partner as the beneficiary for your life insurance policies.

- Name your partner as the beneficiary for your retirement accounts.

- Have the deed of the house in both names with the right of survivorship.

- Make an Advanced Directive, in case you survived and could not speak for yourself, giving your partner the right to make sure your wishes are carried out.

- Have your partner's name on your checking account.

2: A Will Is Not Enough

"It wasn't raining when Noah built the ark."

Howard Ruff

The Unfinished Plan

Gary and Melissa were married at the age of 22 and had three children over the course of 10 years. When the children were four, seven, and nine, they decided to take a trip to celebrate a big promotion that Gary had received. This trip was an adventure. Melissa and Gary were both excited to go to Alaska for two weeks. They were anticipating time without their children to explore our 49th State. This was their first trip alone since their honeymoon. Both Gary and Melissa's parents lived out of State and they had no family nearby. They decided to leave the children with very close friends. They had left the documents necessary to have their children treated in a medical emergency in their absence and thought they had done everything necessary.

They left for Alaska on their long awaited adventure, knowing their children were safe. They were having a wonderful time exploring the state of Alaska and enjoying their time alone. They decided to take a scenic plane tour over the tundra and Mount McKinley. They were enjoying the beautiful scenery and wonderful conversation with their pilot when all of a sudden bad weather came in and the pilot lost control of the plane, resulting in the plane crashing. The pilot, Melissa, and Gary did not survive the crash.

The plane had been equipped with an emergency signal that notified authorities that the plane was in distress. When the authorities were able to identify them, they notified the local police in the town that Melissa and

Gary lived. Names of the victims were not released to the media pending notification to the next of kin. In this case, it was the parents' of both Melissa and Gary.

When the police arrived at the home of Melissa and Gary, they found everything dark. Checking with neighbors, they found out where the children were staying. The police found an address book and were able to locate Melissa's parents and Gary's parents. The police then notified the local authorities in the towns where Gary and Melissa's parents lived. Both sets of grandparents came to their grandchildren as soon as was possible. Upon arriving, they gathered their grandchildren together and told them that their parents had died and how they had died. Knowing that Melissa and Gary had a will, they searched and found it. The problem was when they read the will there was no Guardian named for their children. This usually would mean that the children become wards of the State immediately. Both sets of grandparents were willing to take guardianship of the children. The police had to call the State, to ask permission for the grandparents to take temporary custody of the children. The State agreed and then a Judge had to okay this temporary solution. A hearing before a Judge, took place the following week. Both sets of grandparents wanted to have custody of the grandchildren and the judge did not want the children moved from their home this soon.

They were in a neighborhood that was supportive and the children had friends there. The judge asked if the grandparents would be willing to move into their children's home. Melissa's parents were able to move and not disrupt the children from their home. Gary's parents owned a small business in another State and it was impossible for them to move. The judge gave Melissa's' parents' custody of the three children provided they live in the home that the children were living in now. He gave visiting rights to Gary's parents and they were able to bring them to their home for a month or two each summer. Both sets of grandparents decided to spend Christmas all together. The grandparents got along well and they shared the children as often as possible.

During the long and expensive process of Probate, the Probate Judge appointed Gary's father the executor of Gary and Melissa's estate, because Melissa was the original executor and was now dead. Many things needed to be taken care of. An attorney was hired to place all of Gary and Melissa's assets in a trust for the children.

The undertaking of raising three children for Melissa's parents, a couple beyond their childbearing age, was a huge change in lifestyle for them. They had to disrupt their lives and sell their home to come to another city to take on this life-changing challenge. Everything turned out well in the end. It was very difficult for the children for a very long time and with the love and understanding of their grandparents and some professional counseling, they thrived. The grandchildren and grandparents spoke about Melissa and Gary all the time. They encouraged the grandchildren to express their feelings. How they missed them.

When you are young, you think you will be living a long time. Death does not enter your mind. Yet, many young people die every day.

Death in a family can cause such pain, that those left behind need time to adjust and grieve. This makes it so much more difficult, if the family has all kinds of legal difficulties to straighten out. Each one of us is responsible for what we leave behind. It is never too early to plan and share our wishes.

Things would have been much easier for everyone if planning had taken place at a young age and sharing that knowledge with loved ones.

What can you do to prevent this situation?

- Draft a Last Will and Testament, naming a trusted friend as your executor and naming a guardian for your underage children.

- Have a Trust in place if you have many assets. A Trust does not have to go through Probate process.

- Secure enough life insurance to provide for your children.

- Document your attorney's name and telephone number if any.

- Document your accountants' name and number if any.

- Retirement accounts with a named beneficiary and secondary beneficiaries. (IRA, 401k, Annuities etc.).

Create a binder, folder or large envelope to include:

- Property deeds.

- Mortgage papers if any.

- Loans if any.

- Title to the car(s).

- List of bank accounts.

- Life Insurance Policies if any.

- Retirement accounts.

- Birth certificates.

Disability Woes

Barbie and Chuck

Barbie and Chuck were in their late 40's and had been married for 25 years. They had two children in college. Life was grand and they thought they had it made. Chuck owned a restaurant that was very successful. Barbie and Chuck had worked very hard for the last 10 years to make this restaurant the "go-to" place in town. They each had a will. They named each other as the executor of their wills, and named their oldest daughter as executor if anything were to happen to them at the same time. Their retirement accounts were set up and they thought they had planned well.

Everything was going very well until one day Chuck fell down the basement steps at the restaurant. He was badly hurt and was paralyzed and in a wheelchair. After being released from the hospital, Chuck came home. Chuck was unable to do many of the things that he had done before and it became very difficult for him. He could no longer manage the restaurant and Barbie had to stay home and take care of him. Barbie did everything she could to help. The bills were piling up. They were having staff problems and the business was facing many challenges because neither one of them could be there to direct the business. Barbie tried her hardest to take care of her husband and oversee the restaurant. They did hire a manager for the restaurant but that did not work out.

Things got worse. Chuck diagnosed with a blood clot in his brain, required surgery. He was left, unable to speak and had great difficulty writing. Meanwhile, the restaurant was in a deep decline.

Chuck communicated by writing everything down as well as he could. After much contemplation, Chuck and Barbie decided they would sell the restaurant. They found a broker and put the restaurant up for sale. The broker found someone interested in buying the restaurant. They proceeded with all the paperwork needed. The sale could not go through, for Chuck could not speak for himself. Even though Barbie did a lot for the restaurant, her name was not on the building or the business.

Barbie hired an attorney to go before a judge to declare Chuck incompetent, so that Barbie would have the Financial Power of Attorney, to take over the handling of his affairs. Barbie also had to seek guardianship over her husband. In the State that they live in, if you are unable to speak and walk, you have to be declared incompetent, so that the judge can name someone to speak for you. The legal bills piled up as well.

By this time, they were so far in debt that the building and the business had to be sold immediately. They had depleted all their savings to keep the restaurant open. Eventually they proceeded with the sale of the restaurant and building but did not receive its full value. This whole process took over a year. They were able to keep their home for it did not have a mortgage on it.

Chuck had qualified for disability benefits and Barbie had found a job in the local area. Their two daughters had to find jobs to pay for their education. This whole situation was a disaster and could have been avoided. A will is not enough.

If each of them had a Durable Power of Attorney for both healthcare and finances, they would have been able to carry on much easier. The restaurant and building could have sold much sooner. They would have had less legal bills and a lot less stress.

It was a good thing that, Chuck and Barbie had a will but that was not enough. You never know what life will bring your way. Being prepared can lessen the chaos and financial devastation that can happen to any of us.

What can you do to prevent this situation?

- Have a last Will and Testament.

- Have a DPA (Durable Power of Attorney) for Medical and for Finances.

- Have some sort of Revocable Trust for the Business and building.

- Have a disability insurance policy for the owner of the business.

- Have an Advanced Medical Directive for each of you.

- Purchase life insurance policies.

- Keep all-important documents in the same place.

- Tell someone where the documents are stored.

How do you want to remember your parents?

Jake was an only child. His mother died three years ago from cancer. Jake's father, Ben had handled everything from care giving to funeral arrangements.

Over the last three years, Ben had a hard time with depression and loneliness. Ben was in his 70s, but was quite healthy. Jake tried to assist as often as he could, but had a very busy life with work and family.

One day, Jake received a telephone call to come to the hospital because a neighbor found Ben unresponsive on the sidewalk. The paramedics resuscitated him and transported him to the hospital. Jake arrived at the hospital to find his dad on a respirator (life support). There were tubes and IV's hooked up to monitors that were making all kinds of different noises. This was very hard on Jake.

Jake learned that Ben had suffered a brain hemorrhage and was in a coma. The doctor spoke with Jake about how serious the situation was. Ben did not have a Medical Directive or a Healthcare Proxy. Jake faced making very difficult decisions concerning his father. Did he want his father to undergo brain surgery? He had so many questions. If he were to decide to have his dad undergo the surgery, would he ever come out of this coma? If he did, would he ever be himself again. Would there be brain damage due to the lack of oxygen to his brain? What damage would result? If his dad is removed from life support, he will die. Jake pondered on this for quite a while and came to the decision that they should remove life support. This was the hardest decision of his life.

The doctors removed life support and Jake held his dads' hand and talked to him until he died. Jake was devastated and now had to arrange for his hero. His father did have a will, but the work was only beginning.

After the funeral, Jake had to gather all of his father's important papers and documents. Jake was the executor of Ben's will and had to file the will through the Probate court. This is extremely trying and time consuming, and can be very expensive. Jake did not hire an attorney.

Jake did all the work and coped with grieving as well. He managed his job and cared for his family all at the same time. Jake had his hands full.

He made a list and began checking off what he had to do.

Get certified copies of the death certificate,

Notify Social Security,

Notify Ben's private pension plan,

Notify his life insurance company,

Prepare the paperwork for the probate court,

Decide what to do with the house,

Dispose of his father's personal belongings.

Finally, his father's estate was settled. Many months went by before Jake felt the impact of his father's death. This was a very difficult time for him as he began grieving. Jake questioned whether he had made the best decision or not. If Jake had made the decision to have his father go through the surgery, what would the outcome have been? He struggled with this for quite a while, eventually concluding that his decision was the right one. He could now move forward with his life. As he went through the grieving process, he experienced deep sadness and realized how much he missed his parents. Jake eventually accepted that his parents were at peace but thought of them often.

No one should have to play God and make these decisions for their loved ones. Jake could have hired an attorney to take care of the probate work and saved himself a lot of work and time. This comes with a cost that he did not want to undertake. He felt he needed to do these things not only for his father, but also for himself.

Do you want to remember your parent with love or having left you in a mess requiring you to spend countless hours looking for information that you need to close out accounts, to have the information that you need for a death certificate, information on the background of your parent for an obituary. Please realize that your parents did not intend for you to spend countless hours looking for information on them. People do not realize how many decisions they have to make or how costly they can be both financially and emotionally.

What can you do to prevent this situation?

- Have a Durable Power of Attorney for financial and medical needs.

- Keep all necessary paperwork in one place; deeds, retirement information, Social Security number, parent information, bank account numbers, life insurance policy, loan documents and all other important documents.

- Have an Advanced Medical Directive, stating your wishes and decisions for maintaining life. In other words, do you want to be kept alive by artificial means or do you want comfort care only and let nature take its' course.

- Ideally, prepay your funeral if you can.

Too Young to Decide

Your children will face a real problem, if you are injured and become incapacitated.

Andrew, a 45-year-old male, dropped dead from a heart attack. He was without oxygen for several minutes. His girlfriend Jane had started CPR and when paramedics arrived, they continued CPR for transport to the hospital. The paramedics were not able to get a pulse. They worked on him all the way to the hospital. After 5 minutes in the ER, they finally got a pulse and Andrew continued to stabilize. He was on a respirator and could not breathe on his own. He underwent many tests. He was transported to ICU (intensive care unit), where they performed a procedure that could help minimize brain injury. After the procedure, he was still the same. He was still unconscious and on life support. Jane did not have any say because she was not married to Andrew.

Andrew had a daughter Natalie from a previous marriage and she became the decision-maker for his medical needs for she was now next of kin at age 19. Natalie did not feel she could handle this alone and wrestled with what she could do. She was pretty close to her father and was having feelings she had never had before. She felt lost and scared, confused and very worried. All kinds of questions kept coming up. What if her dad would be left with permanent damage? What would happen if he did not wake up? Would she have to make the decision to keep her dad on life support indefinitely in a nursing facility? She did not know what to do. Natalie was overwhelmed with all that was going on. She felt she could not make the decisions for her father and asked for help from her grandmother, Andrew's mother Ann. Ann was having her own medical issues at this time. Ann agreed and tried to council her granddaughter while her own emotional state was very fragile. After all this was her son.

Andrew's girlfriend Jane could not pay any bills for she could not sign checks on Andrews' checking account. They had lived together for many years, but Andrew had not put Jane on any of his accounts. Jane had a job but could not pay the mortgage or many bills. She was dependent on a 19 year old to make all the decisions. She had absolutely no say.

Andrew had a will but did not have a medical directive or a Durable Power Of Attorney in place. Everything was in limbo.

Andrew did wake up a day later and had suffered brain damage. He was now breathing on his own and removed from life support. There was a long road to recovery ahead.

Andrew was released from the hospital and sent to a Rehabilitation Center. Andrew would undergo therapy to try to get some of the functions back that he lost from the lack of oxygen to his brain, when he had his heart attack. Andrew needed around the clock care. When Andrew came home, his mother and daughter could not take care of him twenty-four hours a day. They hired someone to be with him during the day so that Natalie could work.

Andrew was partially paralyzed and could not walk or speak. Meanwhile, Andrew's mother Ann and his daughter Natalie had to hire a lawyer to present their case to a judge to get control of his affairs and be able to pay the bills. Andrew was declared incompetent by the court, which allowed Natalie and her grandmother Ann, to manage his affairs and to speak for him, making all the financial and medical decisions for him. This is called Guardianship.

Can you imagine being 19 years old and having to take on these responsibilities? Andrew was not a rich man. His daughter had to apply for Medicaid and Social Security Disability and she did so with the help of her grandmother Ann.

Andrew could have named whomever he wanted to make his decisions to see to his financial affairs with a Power Of Attorney for finances and one for his medical care. A will would have made things much simpler in disposing of his property. He could have specified if he wanted a funeral or cremation a service or a celebration of his life. Now it is too late. A person must be of sound mind and able to legibly sign his name to make a will.

How would you decide medical needs for your parents if they are forgetful and have dementia? That qualifies them as incompetent. As our parents are living to an older age and dementia and other life altering events occur, we have the responsibility of seeing to their wishes.

There are so many things to be decided. It could be very trying time and very time-consuming.

What could have been done ahead of time to make this easier on his daughter?

- Andrew could have had a Will drafted or done his own on line.

- He could have had an Advanced Medical Directive to deal with what he wanted for intervention if he had a heart attack or an injury.

- He could have had a Durable Power Of Attorney for finance and named someone other than a 19 year old to oversee his financial affairs.

What can you do to prevent this situation?

- Draft a Will and Last testament

- Organize all-important documents and put in one place.

- Tell someone where everything is.

3: Relationships

"Life is like a game of cards.

The hand that is dealt you represents determination,

The way you play it is free will."

Jawahard Nedru

There is no Agreement amongst Siblings

Paul and Mary went for a ride to the beach. On their way home, a car crossed the yellow line and hit them head on. Paul died instantly and Mary sustained life-threatening injuries. The driver was intoxicated but not injured in the crash and was arrested.

Paul and Mary had four adult children and several grandchildren. The oldest child Danny was the executor of their wills. Paul and Mary expected to live many more years. They were in their late 50's and healthy, plenty of time to set up a trust and inform their children on where everything was and what to do, or so they thought.

The State police called Danny to inform him of the accident and the death of his father and serious injuries to his mother. Danny immediately went to the hospital. The doctor spoke with him and told him his mother was in surgery. He called his three siblings. They all came to the hospital and saw their father and said their goodbyes. They knew their father had a will and everything would go to their mother.

After several hours, their mother was out of surgery but unconscious. The hospital wanted to know what the arrangements were going to be for their father Paul. No one had seen the will and did not know what their father wanted. Death was a subject never discussed in his family. Their mother was still unconscious. They could not agree on a funeral director to handle their father's funeral. The hospital had a window of time as to how long they could keep their father at the hospital for they did not have a large morgue.

The four children were taking turns to be with their mother, who was still unconscious. Danny went to Paul and Mary's home to try to find a will. Danny found a lockbox, but no key. He could not locate any of the papers that he needed.

Danny, returned to the hospital empty handed. Donnie, one of his siblings said they had to decide about funeral arrangements for their father. A bitter argument ensued and no agreement was reached. It left everyone not speaking to each other. They all suffered a horrific loss and were angry, tired, and still very worried about their mother. Finally, Danny stepped up and said that their father would be going to the McConnell funeral home. The call was made and they had an appointment for the next day to arrange things for their dad. This did not please all the siblings.

Arrangements were made for a funeral in three days, with burial in the family plot, hoping their mother would be conscious by then. As it turned out their mother did not regain consciousness for five more days, the funeral went on and they buried their dad still not speaking to each other.

When their mother regained consciousness, she was in a lot of pain. She had some minor brain injury and several broken bones that had required surgery. Danny had to wait another day to tell her that Paul had died instantly in the crash. She kept asking where he was, not really understanding what the children were saying. Finally, it sank in that Paul was dead. She grieved and felt all alone even though her children had rallied around her. She had wanted to see Paul one last time but of course, that was not possible. After many weeks, Mary was finally ready to come home and recuperate. The police interviewed Mary to get information on how the accident happened. The man that had hit them was charged with vehicular homicide. Mary recovered but there was still a rift between the siblings and the story goes on.

Mary now had to go to court for a hearing of the man that caused her injuries and her husband's death. Mary and her four children went to court together and were angry with this man. After many days in court for different hearings and months later, the trial, the man was found guilty of vehicular manslaughter, was sentenced to 17 years in prison and loss of his license forever. During this time, the family was reminded of that terrible day of the accident. Unfortunately, this was not the end. This family had to attend parole hearings over the years and that was very hard as well.

Mary, completely recovered from her injuries, put her affairs in order, so that when she died, all the decisions had been made ahead of time.

Every time you go to court or a parole hearing and see the man that killed your father and hurt your mother, it is as if it all happened yesterday. All the hurt, the blame and feeling of loss, was replayed repeatedly.

Mary died 8 years later from kidney failure. Danny and his siblings eventually became closer again. Life would never be the same again, nor would their relationships. The damage done would last a long time.

In an effort to make things easier on her children when she died.

- Mary set up a Trust and put just about all her assets in it, her house, her car, her stocks, her bank accounts, her furnishings, etc.

- She also drafted a Pour-Over will that allowed anything that was not in the trust at the time of her death, to be part of the trust through Probate

A Revocable Trust does not have to go through Probate.

- Mary signed a Medical Proxy and a Durable Power of Attorney for Finances that she gave Danny in case she became disabled.

Danny was in charge of the Trust and upon Mary's death distributed her assets amongst the four siblings. This allowed all of Mary's assets to pass to the children without going through the Probate process. This saved them a lot of money and time. The house was sold and everyone took what he or she wanted from the house and the remainder was sold.

- Mary also prepaid for her funeral. The children did not have to make any decisions or make any cash outlays.

- Mary had all her documents in one place and everyone knew where they were. With this kind of preparation, it was much easier on her family.

The grieving process can begin much sooner when a person does not have to battle with paperwork for months or hire an attorney.

Mary learned a lot from the death of her husband and made sure that things would be easier for her children when she died.

What can you do to prevent this situation?

- Have a Trust.

- Have a Pour-over will.

- Have a Medical Directive.

- Have a Durable Power of Attorney for finances.

- Have a Prepaid funeral.

- Have all-important documents in one place.

- Make sure someone knows where everything is

A Probate Disaster

Walter, a man in his mid- seventies died suddenly from a massive stroke. He was married and had two adult children. In his early fifties, he left his wife and started his life anew. Legal steps were never taken, such as a separation or divorce. At the time of his death, he was living with his mistress of 25 years. Glory was in her sixties. Walter owned the house that he and Glory lived in. This house had no mortgage. His mistress, Glory also had two children from a previous marriage.

Walter, having done some planning, had a Will. He made a provision in the Will that if he died before Glory, she would be able to stay in his house until she died. He had wanted his mistress Glory to live well after he died and had made provisions in his Will to make that possible. He was a man of some means and put $300,000.00 in Certificates of deposit in his name and Glory's name with the provision of payable upon death of one of them. He had a provision that, upon Glory's death, the remainder of the money and the house, would be divided and given to his and her children.

The house was worth approximately $700,000.00. Since Walter brought all these assets into this relationship, he decided that 75% would go to his children and 25% to Glory's children. Upon Glory's death, the house and the money would go through this formula. Walter had a great relationship with his children and Glory's children.

Walter's mother had died the year before and he received an $80,000.00 inheritance. This check came 1 month before Walter's death. This check was deposited in their joint account until a decision was made on how to invest it. He died before anything of this was done. This was a sizeable estate. The day after his death, Glory went to the bank, cashed in the Certificates of Deposit, and deposited the money in her personal account. Glory now had full control of everything except his car. She was also the beneficiary of his life insurance and retirement fund.

Glories Will did not reflect any of Walter's wishes. The only beneficiaries in her will were her children. Walter's children were not mentioned.

After the funeral, Walter's Will was presented to the Probate Court and was accepted. The only item to be distributed was his car and his house. Due to the provision in his will,

Upon the will becoming a public document, his legal wife and his children filed suit to contest the Will. They would receive nothing because Glory was still living and her will did not follow Walter's wishes. Glory was the executor of Walter's Will.

Walter did not think this through before he died. In his will, Walter should have left to his children whatever inheritance he wanted for them and should have realized that his legal wife had claims on his estate as well.

This case will be in court for years and be very costly.

What could have helped Walter distribute his assets according to his wishes?

- Walter could have consulted an attorney and set up a trust. The trust would own the assets and he could have allowed Glory to remain in the house until her death. It would have allowed his children and her children to inherit if there was anything left.

- He could have divorced his wife many years ago and this would have eliminated another problem.

What can you do to prevent this situation?

- Divorce your legal wife or husband.

- Have a Trust.

- Legally marry your partner.

- Have separate accounts for you and your partner.

- Inform your children about your wishes.

- Place all-important documents in one place.

A Life Changing Event

A young man in his early twenties, Xavier had his life turned upside down in an instant.

Xavier was an only child. When he was born, his father Jeremiah was 49 years old and his mother Gladys was 39 years old. Both parents were thrilled when Xavier was born. They raised him in a small town and saw to all his needs.

Jeremiah was a Science teacher and Gladys was a retired office manager. Jeremiah also owned a small business.

Xavier grew up and moved away to start his own life. He lived about one hour away from his parents.

One Friday night, he called his parents and got the answering machine. He left a message and did not think anything of it. He assumed his parents went off for the weekend as they often did.

Come Monday, he had not heard back from them and called again. There was no answer, just the answering machine. He decided to go check up on them after work. As he approached the house, both cars were in the driveway. When Xavier arrived at the door, his parents' two dogs greeted him. The dogs were very excited to see him.

He went into the house and found his mother on the couch, cold and unresponsive. He called out to his father and got no response. He quickly went upstairs and found his father in his bed, cold and unresponsive.

He called 911 and within five minutes, the police and paramedics arrived. Xavier's parents had been dead for at least two days. Xavier was very distraught and wanted answers from the paramedics and police, as to what could have happened. Of course, they had no answers yet.

The police took Xavier to a neighbor's home and called the Medical Examiner and the Crime Unit. They treated the house and surrounding property as a crime scene. The ME arrived and checked all their medications, and examined their bodies. He could not determine what caused their deaths. The Medical Examiner arranged for both his parents to be transported to the State morgue for autopsy. Xavier was not allowed into the house for two days. He stayed with friends down the road. The Fire Marshall found that a gas leak and that is probably what killed them. The fumes did not affect the dogs, because they had been going in and out through their doggie door. The autopsies verified that Jerimiah and Gladys died from gas poisoning.

Xavier did not know what to do. All the things that Xavier had to do overwhelmed him. He had never attended a wake or been to a funeral in his life. With the help of some friends and family, he was able to locate the name of his father's attorney and accountant.

He knew his father had a will but did not know where it was. Jeremiah kept everything but not in one location. There were numerous file cabinets to go through.

He contacted the attorney who helped him with the arrangements for his parents. The attorney explained to Xavier how to proceed with the filing of his dad's will.

After a week of looking through the file cabinets with the help of friends, he found the will, insurance policies, deeds to their house and other properties, Certificates of deposit, cash and passbook accounts. He also found a box with his parents' passports, birth certificates, SS cards and other pertinent papers.

Xavier was now alone and on his own.

He had so much to do:

Pick up his father's personal belongings from the school.

Get everything he could find in relation to his father's small business and bring it to the accountant and to the attorney.

Attend many meetings with the attorney and the accountant.

Cancel all upcoming appointments that his parents had scheduled.

Clean out the house.

Take care of the dogs.

Xavier was overwhelmed and could not grieve. It still was not real to him. He could not cope with everything. After a period of time, he came to accept the death of his parents. The sadness was very deep.

Xavier was completely surprised when the beneficiary checks came in from his parent's life insurance policies. He knew that all his financial needs would be satisfied.

Xavier began to sell the assets left to him. He felt he could not sell the house because his father had built it. After living in the house for a year or so, he decided that he had to leave. He was in deep depression and had been drinking heavily. After being confronted by the police and charged with DWI, he decided to go into therapy for his depression and alcohol abuse. He had not allowed himself the time to grieve the loss if his parents. He could not get past his anger to begin to heal. Eventually, with therapy, he did begin the grieving process and it was very difficult for him.

Three years after his parent's death and therapy, he met a wonderful woman and he married her ten months later. Xavier is still in therapy and does not drink anymore.

Xavier and his wife bought a small business and are doing very well.

The process was long and difficult and Xavier still thinks about his parents often. Xavier is well on his way to healing but he will never forget.

How could this tragedy have been made easier for Xavier?

Jeremiah should have:

- Created a special place for important documents.

- Told Xavier where the documents were stored.

- Made a list of names and numbers of people his son would have to contact, if something happened to them.

What can you do to prevent this situation?

- Have a Will and or a Trust.

- Have all pertinent documents and information in one place.

- Tell someone close to you where everything is located.

- List the name and number of your accountant.

- List the name and number of your attorney.

- List all of your bank accounts and other money accounts.

- Save business records.

4: The Perfect Case

The Story of a Man Completely Prepared for Death

Alfred and Joan had been married for over 40 years. Both retired, Alfred was a former Military career soldier who had served his country for 30 years. Joan had worked at many jobs over the years, depending on where they were stationed.

They had one child, a girl named Madeline. She was married and had two children Madeline and her husband both were working and their children were thriving.

After Alfred and Joan retired, they settled down in the same state their daughter lived in. They bought a small home and were quite comfortable. Alfred worked part time as a security guard and Joan did volunteer work.

After several years, Joan was diagnosed with cancer. She went through chemotherapy and radiation treatments. She was doing very well for a few years and then the cancer symptoms resurfaced. During the end of her second round of treatment, Alfred was diagnosed with cancer as well. The doctors were managing his cancer as best they could. Alfred was now using a walker to get around and on many different prescribed medications.

Joan normally woke up around 8 A.M. and prepared Alfred's breakfast. On this morning, when she went into the kitchen, her husband was in the doorway, slumped over his walker. Joan called 911 and the police came to the house. Any unattended death (no doctor present), must be responded to. Victim's Inc. was called to come and help in any way that we could. I was the Trauma Intervention Volunteer on call. I immediately went to the house and sat down with Joan, trying to comfort her. Joan was still recovering from her ordeal with cancer was still quite weak. On Joan's behalf, I made phone calls to cancel her husband's appointments and to notify his Doctors of his death.

Any unattended death in our State requires the Medical Examiner be called to determine the circumstances of the death. The police normally stay until the Medical Examiner has left and the deceased is transported to a funeral home. Since Alfred was in his seventies, dying from cancer, there was no need for the Medical Examiner to come to the home for this death was the result of disease.

Joan had called her daughter who was at work. She was two and a half hours away and had to call her husband to pick her up and come to her mother's house.

The police inquired as to what pre arrangements were made, if any. Joan said her husband wanted to be cremated and there were papers somewhere. She was quite upset and could not think of where all the paper work was located. Since the paperwork was not available, the police arranged for Alfred to be transported to the morgue at the local hospital.

The police were able to leave because I was available to stay with Joan. This would free up the police to get back to their other duties.

Joan and I talked about Alfred until her daughter Madeline arrived. I talked with Madeline and she said her Dad had a lock box under his bed. They found the key on the wall.

Everything was in order, keys were marked and on a hook. A list of phone numbers was on the wall in the kitchen. When the box was opened, the first thing to be seen was his service revolver and all the documents needed to take care of everything.

The box contained:

- Alfred's service revolver

- Their prepaid cremation documents.

- Their wills.

- His discharge papers from the Military.

- His and her Social Security cards.

- His Veterans medical card.

- The deed to the house.

- Insurance policies.

- A list of bank account numbers.

- The paid mortgage papers.

- The title to their car.

- Their marriage certificate.

- Their birth certificates.

- The full names of their parents including their dates of birth, dates of death, where they were born and where they died.

- A list of people to notify.

- Other pertinent papers.

- His computer master password.

After everyone received notification that Alfred had died, I commented on how well organized Alfred was. Joan said, "He had always been like that since the day they were married. He never knew when he would be deployed and was always ready."

Joan was weepy and I tried to comfort her. Madeline and her husband packed up some of her mother's things and they took her home with them.

A memorial service was held a week later.

Being prepared made it so much easier for Joan and Madeline. There was still a lot to do but it was not overwhelming. Alfred was prepared, allowing his family to begin to mourn and not have the burden of having to find everything they needed.

We want to remember our parents with love and appreciation. Sometimes that is hard to achieve, when documents are not in place and preparation is not done for their deaths.

As people age, dementia and Alzheimer's disease is prevalent. With dementia or Alzheimer's, people are not capable of making proper decisions. If both of your parents are living now, enjoy them. Please get the information you need before they die.

Ask them to make the following and let you know where the information is:

- A will

- An Advanced Directive

- A Durable Power of Attorney for finances.

Please get the history of your family. Get your parents to compile your family's history that includes your grandparent's names (maternal and fraternal), their birthdates, where they were born, and their dates of death and where they died. Some of this information is necessary in most States to obtain a death certificate.

Encourage your parents to do this now while they are healthy. You should do it too! Preparation for death will be of great help to those you leave behind who will have to communicate what you wanted, what you have and to whom you wanted it to go. The proper documents will relieve your loved ones from making the decisions themselves on medical directives, decisions that may end your life. The burden of guilt is a heavy one. Do not force this on a loved one.

Send Me the Flowers Before You Die

Do it sooner than later

Protect your rights to make your own decisions.

Make your own decisions known to family members and your attorney, saving someone else trying to second-guess what you want.

Distribute your material goods to whomever you please in an updated Will. Do not leave these decisions to the Probate court.

Hire an experienced attorney to create the documents.

A Will and or a Trust. (Depending on your circumstances).

A Durable Power of Attorney for Finances.

A Living Will or Advanced Directive.

Demonstrate your love for those you hold dear.

The more you do in advance of need, the less your loved ones will have to undertake. Proper preparation eliminates the potential for family disputes over what to do.

Minimize Professional Fees.

Organize your personal information so that all is in order and accessible. This will minimize the cost to your loved ones. Not having to hire an attorney will save a lot of money.

Deal with the reality of death as an unscheduled event.

Make your own funeral arrangements ahead and prepay it. If this is not possible, write down how you want things to be done.

Do you want to have a funeral?

Do you want to be cremated?

Do you want a public or private wake?

Where do you want to be buried?

Do you have a burial plot? If so, locate the contract and include it with your important documents.

What Funeral Home do you want to use?

Do it sooner than later, by sending them the flowers before you die.

5: End of Life Planning

"By failing to prepare, you are preparing to fail"

Benjamin Franklin

We all die at some point, ready or not. End of life planning is more than having an advanced care plan for medical decisions. It must also address legal, emotional and financial matters. Start the end of life planning process by having a conversation with your family. It is easier to plan when you are healthy, alert and able to make decisions for yourself.

For the love and benefit of your loved ones, START a conversation now.

We, as a culture, put off planning or even discussing our end of life wishes. The most common arguments are:

It is just too big to put your arms around.

No clue where to start.

It is too complicated and overwhelming.

It is too big a mess to sort out.

When you die, as we all will, your family will be in an emotional turmoil. They will feel overwhelmed by the task of closing out your estate. Advanced planning is a gift to your family that should be done. When we are prepared, it decreases their feelings of being overwhelmed by everything. For our own death, we are able to relieve the decision making burden (and it is a burden) on those we love and create a peace filled end of life.

The guessing games and struggles over medical treatments, decisions on your behalf that your family will go through, could all be avoided or drastically reduced with proper planning. There would be less heartache, if we would only face the reality that life ends. Documenting your preferences is really a great gift to those you love. Taking care of business, as they say, is so rewarding. Knowing you are doing everything in your power to make it easier on your loved ones is a liberating process. This is not something you do because it is fun. You do it as an act of love for yourself and those you leave behind. Proper planning results in less pain and anguish for your family because you made your own decisions. You have been making your own decisions for most of your life. Why stop now? Take some time to sort this all out and decide what you want.

Do not rush to try to do everything at once.

- Start by taking the time to clarify your feelings and attitudes about dying and death.

- What would you like to have as your final goodbye?

- Do you want a public wake or a private wake?

- Do you want a private funeral or a public funeral?

- Are there any special songs you want played?

- Is there a special person you want to perform the funeral?

- Where do you want to be buried?

- Would you rather be cremated?

- Do you have a burial plot?

- Would you still want a memorial service?

- Would you prefer a celebration of your life instead of a wake?

- Would you want your ashes disposed of in a certain way?

- Do you have a favorite charity that people could send donations to in your memory?

- How will you pay for your funeral?

- Do you have a life insurance policy to pay for your funeral?

- Do you have enough money to prepay your funeral?

- If you have the resources, it is a good idea to see a funeral director and pay for it now. This applies to people who are over 50 years of age.

- After you have thought through these points, write down your wishes.

- Incorporate your wishes in your Will and decide on an Executor. If you do not have a will, please consider creating one now.

- What are your assets and personal items?

- What are your assets?

- Make a list and decide if special items will go to special people. These special gifts should be listed in your Will noting the persons to receive them.

- Make sure your money accounts have a beneficiary as well as your retirement funds and life insurance.

- Name a beneficiary for the remainder of your assets, furniture etc.

- You can make a simple Will on line. (Google free wills.)

- Make a Living Will to choose how you want to live the end of your life.

- Make a Durable Power of Attorney for Healthcare

- Make a Durable Power of Attorney for Finances.

- Think things through and then let someone know where these documents are.

- Be sure to ask the people you have chosen to serve as your agents if they are comfortable with this role.

A Special Gift.

Something else you can leave as a very special gift for your children and grandchildren is a journal of all the things you remember about your grandparents, parents and your childhood. You can recall things your children did growing up. You can recall special moments. You can document anything you want to. This would be greatly appreciated by your family.

The world is changing every day and not one of your grandchildren or maybe even your children know what it was like before TV, DVR's Video, Cell Phones, Computers, and Tablets etc. Technology is in every facet of our lives today.

Write some stories about how you spent your time growing up without all these gadgets. I love all these gadgets and use many of them but I want my grandchildren to know things seemed simpler when I grew up.

We had freedom as children that certainly could not happen today. In the summer, after getting up in the morning and having breakfast, we were outside, all over the neighborhood until the street lights came on. We did come in to eat when called. We played ball, rode our bikes etc. We developed friendships and spoke to each other. We ate dinner at the table and had conversations with our parents. Our memories may not seem important to us but it can be a revelation for our children and grandchildren.

Try it. It is fun and brings back some wonderful experiences.

6: After the Death comes GRIEF and BEREAVEMENT

"Death ends a Life but not a Relationship"

Mitch Album

Death is a pre-existing condition that we all succumb to one day. For those left behind, grief will begin.

Grief is an emotional process of reacting to a loss of a loved one who has died. Grief is normal and necessary. Grief is what we feel inside ourselves to a connection that has been lost. The connection can be with a loved one, a friend, someone you have had a connection with in your life. We feel numbness and disbelief, emptiness, yearning and despair.

We feel distressed because of the lost connection. Most of the time, this is due to a loved one dying but can also be reflected in a divorce, loss of a pet or many other situations.

Grief is painful and you may feel overwhelmed and feel this is too much to handle.

For your own wellbeing, you must experience and feel the effects of grief. Let it flow through you and claim it. This process can be short or very long. The only way out of pain is going through it. We cannot heel what we do not feel. Allow yourself these feelings and express them. Cry all you want, be angry, it is natural and okay.

Grief is a highly individualized experience. How you react depends on many factors,

- Your personality and coping style,

- Life experiences,

- Faith and beliefs,

- The nature of your loss.

- Grief is a slow process and cannot be hurried or forced.

- Grieving is very exhausting. You may feel foggy, not remember things, feel you no longer can cope with some things and have headaches or chest pain.

- This is due to the grief's physical impact on the brain. This is temporary but can last for several months. Be patient.

Many people never stop grieving the death of a loved one, especially a child. Grief is a response to feelings and you slowly adjust to those feelings. Learning to grieve is in part instinct.

Grief is also called Bereavement. Grief or Bereavement is different from Mourning.

Mourning is what we do to show our grief, crying, being angry, and wearing black for a period. Grief is a highly individual visualized experience. Grief is the emotional component that can make you feel overwhelmed.

Healing takes place after you experience the anger you feel. There are no shortcuts. You do not get over grieving; you slowly adjust and learn to live with it.

Each of us is unique and we will express our grief in different ways. Grief can affect you emotionally, physically, mentally and spiritually. There is no time limit on grief.

Be gentle with yourself and patient for it can take a long time to heal. Tell yourself you will survive. Numbing the pain with alcohol and drugs are not the answer. Grief is not a major pressure. Grief is a normal occurrence in our lives. It hurts and is painful.

As Dr. Monica Murphy says," Grief is like riding on a roller coaster. You will have a few days when you think the worst is over and the pain almost bearable and then you slide back into being really down especially in the first year after your loss when birthdays, holiday's anniversaries and special occasions come up. "Life is fleeting and fragile. Live, love, as though every day is your last or your mother's or your child's last day. Leave no word unsaid, leave no plans unmade."

When you are grieving, people around you are uncomfortable for they fear death. They may even make insensitive comments like "I understand how you feel. " No, they do not. Grieving is so personal and different for each one of us. It is essential to grieve as fully and as long as it takes. Understand that people mean well but do not understand the healthy grieving process. People, who do understand, will silently stand by you and not attempt to interfere with your grief.

Healing begins to take place after you experience the anger and despair. You will question yourself. Could you have done more or said more to a loved one that died? There are no shortcuts. Each one of you is unique and will express your grief in a different way.

Steps you can take in your healing and regaining a sense of stability.

- Take care of yourself. Allow people to help you in some of the more difficult tasks that seem overwhelming, like going through the belongings of your loved one or getting errands done, making appointments, etc.

- Eat right.

- Get enough sleep.

- Talk to people you trust and share your feelings.

- Join a grief group. There are numerous websites to help you as well.

- Do not use alcohol or drugs to numb the pain.

Signs that someone grieving may need professional help.

A person who is very sensitive to the loss can become very agitated or anxious about death. A person who develops compulsive behavior. A person who shows no emotional expression. A person who lacks the basics of self-care.

Professional counseling can help move this person through their grief.

As you start to adjust without your loved one, your life becomes a little better and more organized. Your physical symptoms become less and depression begins to lift slightly. As you become more functional, your mind starts working again and you can find solutions to the problems you face. You may begin to heal by reconstructing yourself and your life without your loved one. You will learn to deal with and accept the reality of a new normal and find a way to move forward. You will start to look forward to planning. You will be able to think about your loved one without the extreme pain and sadness and eventually find some joy in the experience of living.

According to the experts, there are five stages of grief.

Stage I: Denial

Denial is disbelief, numbness, and shock. This provides emotional protection from being overwhelmed all at once. This may last for weeks. You may find yourself saying, "This just can't be happening to me".

Stage II: Anger and Guilt

Anger is blaming others or yourself. Who was to blame, God, yourself, the doctor, etc.? You may have the need to blame someone for what has happened. You may be angry with the person who died for abandoning you.

You may feel guilty about things you did or did not do or things you said or did not say.

Stage III: Bargaining

Bargaining is saying," Do not let this be happening to me. I will be more involved or I will do better."

Stage IV: Depression

Depression is a long period of sad reflection that will overtake you. Encouragement from others is not helpful at this time. It is at this time that you realize the full magnitude of your loss and it depresses you. You may feel anxious, hopeless or insecure. This profound sadness is the most experienced sign of grief

Stage V: Acceptance

Acceptance is coming to terms with the loss and being at peace with what happened. Accepting the fact that your loved one will not be at the dinner table for celebrations.

Not everyone goes through all the stages of grief and that is perfectly fine. The stages of grief do not happen in any particular order and some stages can be missing.

Do not grieve alone.

Lean on people care about you, your loved ones and good friends.

If you follow, religious traditions embrace the comfort of spiritual activities, praying and meditating.

Join a support group sharing your loss with others also can help.

Face your feelings. In order to heal, you must face and bear your pain.

Write about your loss in the Journal or write a letter to your loved one that you lost.

Make a scrapbook of all your memories of your lost love one.

Get involved in a cause.

Take care of your physical health.

Find moments of joy and laugh.

Prepare yourself for emotional times, holidays for anniversaries and special occasions.

It may take you more than a year to overcome strong feelings of grief and totally accept the loss. Grief should not be prevented. It is necessary to begin the healing process.

Things to say to someone in Grief:

- I am sorry for your loss.

- I wish I had the right words, just know that I care.

- I do not know how you feel but I am here to help in any way that I can.

- My favorite memory of… is….

- I am always just a phone call away.

- Say nothing and give that person a hug.

- Say nothing just be with the person.

Worst things to say:

- At least he or she lived a long life.

- He or she is in a better place.

- At least he or she is not suffering anymore.

- You must be strong.

- He or she was such a good person, God wanted he or she to be with him.

Death of a child:

In most cases, parents find the grief unbearably devastating when having lost a child. This is a lifelong process for them. Parents never get over the death of a child. They learn to live with the loss. The trauma of losing a child is very significant the feelings of shock, guilt, anger and deep sadness can be overwhelming. It is hard to imagine the depth of pain caused by this loss. The anger maybe such as you has never felt before. Crazy thoughts and finding yourself doing strange things, which have you thinking that you are going crazy. Grief of losing a child is a lifelong process, as parents do not get over the death they just learn to live with it. Losing a child may results in family breakups or suicide.

Journaling can give you a safe place to record your feelings and what is in your heart.

Death of a spouse:

Many people who have lost a spouse feel they have lost a big part of themselves. It is important that you ask for help from family and friends, to do the things your spouse normally did, until you can carry out these tasks yourself. The adjustments that you have to make can be difficult. Taking over tasks that your spouse was responsible for can be overwhelming. Ask good friends to help you, by doing errands for you or just listening.

Death of a sibling:

This is a devastating life event for a sibling especially as an adult. The sibling relationship is considered the longest significant relationship in their lives. Siblings who have been part of each other's lives since birth such as twins help form and sustain each other's identities. This results in the loss of that part of the survivor's identity. The sibling relationship is unique for they share a special bond and genetic traits and a common history.

Death of a parent:

A child who loses a parent to death may have long-term psychological problems if they do not have support to manage the effects of their grief.

Adult children, who lose a parent in midlife, may be impacted in different ways. An adult child may seek out a friend or shun them while trying to process the loss of someone they have known all their lives. An adult child may evaluate his for her own life more closely. Adult children may look at their own mortality more closely. A failure to accept and deal with the loss will only result in further pain and suffering.

Arranging for your own death relieves some of the pressure on your children and loved ones, who are now in grief. Making plans in advance for your funeral and paying for it will ensure your wishes are carried out. Doing this in advance will cause less confusion and cost to your loved ones. Making decisions for the funeral or cremation is very difficult in this time of grief.

Send them the flowers before you die and make it easier for your family.

Supporting a grieving friend or loved one at special times of the year.

Do not be afraid to acknowledge the loss of a loved one.

Holiday's, anniversaries, birthdays and special occasions may be very difficult for the grieving person. Just letting someone know you are thinking about him or her at this time will let him or her know you care.

Listen and allow the tears to flow. Encourage the grieving person to talk about the loved one who has passed away. Invite her or him to join the holiday gathering if they are alone.

Send a card and be sure to mention the deceased.

Visit the cemetery with that person.

Offer your help, listen and be there for the grieving person.

Traumatic and complicated grief:

Traumatic grief is defined as grief from **traumatic** event. The traumatic event could be a death from violence, mutilation or multiple deaths such as a car accident or fire.

The symptoms of traumatic grief are similar to posttraumatic stress disorder (PTSD).

Professional help is probably needed in these situations.

Grief in children:

Children are often the forgotten mourners. Their needs are honestly overlooked in the emotional turmoil.

Children grieve differently from adults.

Adults feel that not confronting the issue head-on with children is the path to take. Parents think they are protecting their children from the pain. They just do not think children are able to understand death and therefore are not deeply affected. Wrong. This will not work and may have an adverse effect the child later in life.

If you explain death in terms that they understand, they will get. It.

Sensitivity and honesty will help children process their own grief in a healthy way. It is important for children to feel full emotions and experience all stages of grief as it is for an adult.

Never play down a child's grief. Listen to them and let them cry all they want and need to.

Encourage your child to talk about their painful emotions and let them speak freely. Stifling them can result in emotional problems later on in life.

As painful as it is to watch, your child must learn to cope with loss and tragedy.

Do not let your children grieve alone. Encourage them to reminisce about a lost love one. Have them tell stories about the time they spent with a lost love one. Both good and bad.

Let the child see you cry so that they know it is okay for them as well. Reassuring them that no matter how sad you are, you still love them, will care for them and keep them safe.

Do not tell the child not to feel bad or to stop crying. You would not say that to an adult so why say that to a child.

Do not try to make a child feel better by keeping them busy. Although this just postpones the grieving process.

It is important for children to feel painful emotions and experience grief in all stages.

Do not add to their burden by turning them into your confidant.

If you asked your child" how do you feel about grandma dying?" You will receive the following answer, "I'm okay".

A better way to talk to a child is to speak openly and honestly about their lost love one. Say, "Boy, I sure am sad that grandma died. I will miss her cookies, hugs and kisses. "Do you"? You can cry and hug each other.

Answer all their questions honestly about the death of a loved one. Children's imaginations tend to bring images of what happened that are a lot scarier than the truth.

Let us say grandma died in a car accident when a truck hit her. She hit her head so hard that she died. It is extremely important to use the word dead or died no matter what age the child is. If you say to a four-year-old that daddy went to sleep and did not wake up instead of saying daddy died or daddy is dead, this child may very well have many terrifying and sleepless nights, afraid that he or she may experience the same thing.

Children do not understand the phrases; passed on, no longer with us, went to sleep and will not wake up or God has taken daddy or grandma to heaven.

Encourage the child to ask any questions they have about death. If you listen closely, you will know how to answer simply or in detail.

Children are curious and may want to know what happens to the person after they die. They may ask," Are they hungry"? "Are they cold"? " How do they go to the bathroom"?.

Answer honestly that when a person has died, their body and mind no longer work anymore. They cannot talk, think, walk or move for they have died. Their body was broken so badly that it could not be fixed.

If you believe in the spiritual hereafter, you may tell the child that we all have a special soul or spirit in us and when someone dies that person's spirit or soul is no longer in their body. Tell them the spirit of that person leaves their body when they die and goes to heaven but their body stays here.

If you say to a child that "Daddy went to heaven", they believe that daddy's cold body went to heaven, not his spirit. The child may want to die to be with daddy. The child can live in fear, thinking the angels of God may come to get him or her.

You can explain to a child that heaven is a wonderful place that is for all souls or spirits. Let them know that you cannot see heaven feel it or visit their. It is only for souls.

Should a child go to the wake or the funeral?

A child over the age of five or six should be given the opportunity to attend the funeral. Give them the option of going but do not force it. A funeral service helps affirm that the loved one is actually dead and is going to be buried. It provides some amount of closure and needed support from family and friends. A funeral service exposes children to the process and ritual of it. It helps them understand that death is final. It is okay to feel that they can mourn as others are doing.

Prepare your child by explaining what they will see and what happens and that people may be crying. If it is an open casket, tell them what daddy will look like. Let them choose whether they want to see that person or not.

You may want to get the book, "Tear Soup" by Pat Schiverbert. This book is written in children's book format with simple concepts. This book gives as much to adults as it does to grieving children of all ages.

Age specific grieving:

Toddlers (less than three years old).

Toddlers may miss a loved one but they cannot grasp the concept of death. They do not understand the difference between an absence and a permanent loss.

Grieving, in toddlers, can present itself by frequent crying, acting out, fuzziness, clinging to a parent, changes in sleeping and eating and or regression to thumb sucking or in toilet habits.

You can help toddlers by trying to maintain a normal routine and surroundings, which is difficult due to your own grief. Provide a lot of hugs and kisses. Even toddlers have to be told that daddy died and will not be coming back. This is extremely hard to do but it is necessary. Have a picture of the loved one near when speaking to the child about daddy or other loved ones.

Preschool (3 to 5-year-olds)

Preschoolers have a perception of death that is temporary and reversible (only a separation). They may ask repeatedly "When is daddy coming home"? They may show fear returning to daycare. They can act out and throw temper tantrums and regress to a more immature behavior. They may even think their thoughts and feelings caused the death.

Explaining death in the simple way that allows them to know they will never see, speak to or hold daddy ever again. Make sure they understand they were in no way responsible for daddy's death.

Tell them you will love them, take care of them and keep them safe always.

Middle childhood (6 to 9-year-olds)

Children of this age have a clearer idea of death. They may still confused death with sleep. They do not understand the finality of death and find it hard to separate life and death.

Discuss the death using the words died or death.

Provide simple explanations to the questions. Tell the truth but not a lot of details. Tell them the importance of feelings and encourage crying. Encourage questions and let them know you will never leave them. Let them participate in the memorials, activities, and projects that follow.

Preteens (10 to 12 years old)

At this age, children begin to understand that death is final. They may worry about their own safety. Death scares them and they are just starting to understand their own mortality.

They may have a hard time concentrating and may do poorly in school. They may ask specific questions about death, the body and funerals. Talk openly and honestly about the death, the body in any specifics the past for. Let them feel in crying and expressing their grief to you. It is okay to cry with them.

Encourage them to express the grief through writing, music and art. You can do this as well and it might help a little bit.

Let the child create his or her own memorial celebration or planting a tree or anything that he or she may want to do is say goodbye.

Teens

Teenagers perceive death in much the same way adults do. They may react by misbehaving or acting out. They may engage in dangerous activities in an attempt to defy death.

Being a teenager is already hard and adding grief to their situation becomes a significant burden. Teens have suicidal thoughts and see death as a romantic event.

Peer influence is so important at this age that teens may resent and feel embarrassed about death. They may feel different or isolated from their peers. They may try to turn off the grief they may act as if nothing happened but are truly torn up inside.

Do not force them to talk about the death. You may want to start a conversation on how you feel about the death. Be a good listener and acknowledge their grief without criticism. Let them know it is normal to cry and feel extreme sadness, guilt and regret.

Support groups for teens can be very helpful.

Watch carefully for any signs of suicidal tendencies or depression that worsen over time.

Suicidal signs or tendencies:

- Making suicidal statements,

- Being preoccupied with death in conversation, writing or drawing.

- They give away prized belongings.

- They withdraw from family and friends.

- Hostile behavior.

- Neglecting personal appearance.

- Running away from home.

- Reckless behavior; reckless driving.

- A change in personality from upbeat to quiet.

- If you notice any of these signs, please get your child professional help immediately. Let them know you care and love them.

"Grief never ends…. However, it changes. It is a passage, not a place to stay. Grief is not a sign of weakness, nor a lack of faith…. It is the price of love."

-Author Unknown-

7: What is a Last Will and Testament?

> "If you have built castles in the air,
>
> Your work need not be lost.
>
> That is where they should be.
>
> Now put foundations under them"
>
> Henry David Thoreau

People used to think that a Will was just for the rich or those with many assets and properties. That is not the case. Any homeowner or investor risks losing their assets to the government, if they do not make definite plans for inheritance. To protect your assets and provide for your family, a Will needs to be on your agenda.

A Will and Last Testament is a legal document detailing the allocation or disposition of all your assets after you die according to the instructions given while you were alive.

You can specify how you want to distribute your assets.

You can specify what you want for final arrangements.

You will name an executor to manage your assets during the probate process.

If you have young children, you can name a guardian for them.

If you have property in another state, (ex. summer home) your will may have to be filed in that state as well.

If you are married, you should each have your own will.

Probate is the legal process of overseeing the transfer of assets. After death has occurred, a Will is presented to the Probate Court along with many forms. A Will must be probated before it can become valid. All assets are frozen during this time. (Not able to be sold or distributed).

Exceptions to the rule:

- Your Spouse inherits without going through Probate.

- Jointly owned property does not go through Probate. (House, Vacation Home or Condo, CD's, Bank Accounts).

- Life insurance policies with a defined beneficiary, 401 k plans or retirement accounts, again with a named beneficiary. etc., do not have to be probated.

If you do not have a Will, it is called having Died Intestate. This also requires that the forms be completed for the Probate process and a Judge will decide who gets what. This is a long process and can be very expensive.

Note: The only mechanism to name a guardian for your children under 18 is in a will.

To write a will, the following elements must be present:

- You must be of legal age to make a Will.

- You must be of sound mind.

- You must be able to sign the will voluntarily and in a valid way.

A Will consists of several clauses:

Funeral expenses and payment of debts; this is where you place pertinent information regarding how your funeral expenses and other debts will be paid through your estate. In this clause, you can also forgive debts someone owes you.

Gifts of personal property; this is where you state how you would like your material possessions divided.

Gifts of real estate; this is where you state your division of real estate.

Residuary clause; this will cover all assets not specifically disposed of by the will. This clause distributes assets that you might not have anticipated owning.

Naming a Guardian, this is where you would nominate a guardian for any child of yours, less than eighteen years of age.

Naming an Executor, this is where you would name an executor or personal representative, who will take charge of your personal property after you die. The Executor will submit your will to the probate court.

Consult an experienced attorney to make sure you are following your State guidelines.

You can also "Google" the term "Free Wills" and get a lot of information at numerous sites.

Executing a Will makes it easier for your family and friends to navigate State laws. A Will is a legal document that you can draw- up online or sees an attorney to draw it up for you or you can write your own Will. (Check your State law, as a hand written Will is not recognized in some states).

In your Will, you can specify how you want your remains taken care of. You can choose to be cremated and have a service, have your ashes buried in the cemetery, or be given to someone you love. You can choose to have a wake or a service and burial or a combination of any of the above or if you do not want a service. You may choose to have a gathering in celebration of your life. If there are special customs in your culture or religion, you may specify those in your Will. A benefit of a Will is you have the ability to choose.

A Will is truly your Last Testament to your instructions on how you want things to be done. You may want to give your body to medical science. You may want to give some of your organs to help others or even save their lives. It is your choice but if no one knows your wishes beforehand, it is up to whoever is your next of kin. Few people arrive at the hospital after someone dies with that person's will in hand, even if they know where everything is. This is why a will is not enough.

A Will can also distribute assets to the people you choose and certain items of value to other people close to you. Let us say you have an antique Corvette. You want your grandson to have at age 21. This can be specified if you so choose. You can also specify at what age you want your child or children to inherit your estate. Complete control could be at age 25 or 30. Below that age, the Trustee would distribute money for your children for their care or for anything that they needed, such as money for their education, etc.

You must have an Executor for your will. Make sure you choose someone you trust who can oversee what your wishes are and carry them out in the manner you set forth.

A Will is presented to the Probate Court to verify that the Will is legal. All assets are frozen until the judge has an accounting of your possessions and your creditors have come forward and been paid off.

A Will makes sure things are distributed the way you want them to be. If no one knows about this, or has a copy of it, nothing will go the way you wanted it to.

A Will, when it is filed with the court, becomes a public document.

What is a Pour–Over Will?

> "I am prepared for the worst,
>
> But hope for the best."
>
> Benjamin Disraeli

A Pour-Over Will is a legal form created to manage assets or property that is not in the Trust. A Pour-Over Will allows you to put any assets you may have forgotten that are not in the Trust into the trust upon completion of Probate. This will has to go through Probate to be validated. The assets that you have forgotten to include in your Trust can be turned over to the Trust immediately after probate. This means that the assets you forgot to put into the Trust are frozen until probate is over. This can be a short time or a long time, depending on what has to be done.

The biggest advantage to a Pour-Over Will in conjunction with a Trust is that you are in charge of all of your assets until you die.

8: What is a Trust?

"Death does not wait to see if things are done or not done."

Kularnova

A Trust is a legal document that provides a direct line for inheritance that does not involve an attorney or court to be involved after your death. The time factor is minimal in comparison to a will and grants your family a lot less cost and frustration. It also gives you peace of mind, knowing everything is in place, allowing your loved ones to grieve and celebrate your planning for them.

A Trust is a legal document that is private and does not have to go through the Probate process. There are no public records of your Trust.

A Trust enables you to protect your assets from being a target for people or family that want to cause havoc for your loved ones at a time when they are most vulnerable.

If you own a business, a Trust allows the continuation of the business without interruption. The business can be sold if necessary.

With a Trust, there is no waiting period. None of your assets is under the control of a judge or court. Some estates take years to be sorted out due to lack of planning and can be a great financial and emotional burden on your family. A Trust can do practically anything you want it to do. There are hundreds of clauses that can be tailored to your unique situation.

A Trust is not for everyone. You may not need a Trust if you do not have a business or have many assets.

The Elements of a Trust.

Four primary elements make up the structure of a trust. Every trust must have these four elements.

Trust Maker: The person making the trust. Other names attributed to the Trust Maker are the "Grantor" or "Settlor".

Trustee: The Trustee is a person you name to oversee your Trust and distribute your assets according to the terms of the Trust. This person sometimes can be the Trust maker. This Trustee should be someone you trust. Usually, this is your spouse or adult child, or it can be a professional, such as an Attorney or Institutional Trustee.

Trustees are legally required to act as Fiduciaries (a person who holds something in trust for another). This is the highest standard of responsibility under the law.

Successor Trustee: When the original Trustee dies or is no longer able to perform his or her duties, then the Successor Trustee will take over the Trust and all the responsibilities that go with it.

The Trustee, after your death, will file the Trust with the State. The Trustee will oversee the distributions of your assets to the beneficiaries in accordance with the terms of the Trust.

Beneficiaries: Name of the person or persons who will benefit from the existence and operation of the trust are called the beneficiaries. Sometimes the Trust Maker is the beneficiary. After the Trust Maker dies, normally the spouse or children become the beneficiaries.

Trust Corpus: The assets and body of the trust are known as the Trust Corpus. These elements are interdependent. No trust can exist if one of these elements is not included.

Trust Clauses.

Every trust consists of a series of paragraphs or groups of phrases called clauses. Clauses are tools to make sure the trust makers have everything they want in the trust. There are widely used clauses that can be in almost any trust. Here are a few examples:

Mental Competency Clause.

This clause instructs the Successor Trustee to have the original Trustee examined if there is serious concern about that person's competency. The Successor Trustee can have that person examined by a doctor, a neurologist and a psychologist to determine competency. The point of this clause is to avoid the public nature of a competency hearing. If the person is found to be incompetent, the Trusteeship automatically passes to the Successor Trustee.

No Contest Clause.

This clause clearly states that any beneficiary of the Trust, who challenges the distribution of the Trust, will automatically be punished by losing a part or all of their inheritance. This is usually is used to discourage any disgruntled heirs or their spouses to challenge the trust.

Mediation/Arbitration Clause.

All disputes are handled in this way through a third party. A neutral party will gather both sides of the issue at hand and negotiate a settlement.

Spendthrift Clause.

Protects the heirs' inheritance from their own creditors. A third party controls the inheritance.

Distributions to Minors Clause.

This clause instructs the trustee how to manage funds for the benefit of a minor.

Distribution to disabled person clause.

This clause instructs the trustee how to manage and distribute the funds for a disabled person.

Powers and duties of Trustee clause.

This clause explains the duties of the Trustee.

Since the Trust comes into effect as soon as if it is funded, there is no freezing of the assets like with a Will. All assets are available in a very short time. **Any asset that has a Deed or a Title must be in the name of the Trust.**

When you put assets into a Trust, you no longer own those assets. For example, a piece of land is deeded to the XYZ Revocable Trust. Once this is accomplished, it is safe from probate. Upon your death and according to the terms of the Trust, your property will pass on to your named beneficiary or beneficiaries. Since you no longer own the assets, those assets are harder to be considered by creditors. All Control of your assets and money are directly under your control until you die. You can designate what assets are to go to a specific person or persons.

You can specify any provision that you want except naming a guardian for minor children.

A Will, is the only place you can name a guardian for a minor child. If you do not do this, your children can become wards of the state. The state will be responsible for your children. A judge will have to decide who will bring up your children rather than you. It can cause arguments among aunts and uncles who come forward to raise the children.*

A Trust can shelter assets for your spouse, from federal and state estate taxes, and from other concerns such as a divorced spouse that remarried etc. A Trust allows for as many of the assets as possible, to go to the intended beneficiaries directly.

If you have a business, the shares of stock must be in the name of the Trust.

It is best to list everything you own or list categories like collectibles, all personal, property, jewelry and specific items that are to go to a particular person. Many times when people buy a new car, they forget to put the tittle in the name of the Trust. This car is not included in the trust and must go through Probate Court via the pour-over will.

A Trust is designed to pass your assets to your heirs directly upon your death. Trusts are established in the State of residency of the person setting up the trust. With a Trust that is funded, you can control distribution of your assets according to the design of the trust document. Assets placed in a Trust, will be excluded from the Estate after death. Trusts are harder to contest than a will. You can also have Sub Trusts under the umbrella of the main trust.

It is recommended that your checking accounts and savings be put in the name if the Trust. The name of the Trust does not have to appear on the check but should be reflected on the paper work at the bank. This will help protect your cash at a higher level.

All other assets like furniture should be put in categories and be included in the Trust. You can do this with a bill of sale or bill of transfer, written in very broad terms, to the Trust.

In Simpler terms, you will need:

- A person or persons to establish the Trust.

- A Trustee to manage the Trust.

- A Successor Trustee in case the primary trustee cannot perform his or her duties.

- Named beneficiaries of the assets.

- Funds for the trust. Funding the Trust is by putting assets in the name of the Trust.

- Run and support a business without interruption.

- Addresses instructions for the care of minors in the distribution of funds.

- Pay Medical bills.

- Create a Scholarship Fund.

- Hold real estate, cash, securities, and other assets.

- Avoid Probate.

- Save Federal Taxes.

- Hold assets together for future instructions.

- Protects assets from of creditors' reach

- Protects property and assets from a prior divorce.

- To provide for a disabled child or relative.

- To keep assets for future generations.

There are four major types of Trusts.

Revocable Trusts.

A Revocable Trust can be, amended, added to, removed from or revoked during the Trust Makers' lifetime. After the death of the trust maker, this type of trust becomes irrevocable.

You can make changes any time while you are living.

You can change Trustees at any time.

You can buy and sell assets at any time.

Irrevocable Trusts.

No changes to an Irrevocable Trust are allowed to be made once the Trust has been written up and signed. Of course , if the Trust is not funded, it is of no consequence. Funding, once it is in this type of Trust, cannot be removed or sold, unless cash replaces the item or property in it's' place.

This trust can be used to fund legacies for children or grandchildren.

This trust can also be used to make gifts of property and other assets.

Testamentary Trusts.

A Testamentary Trust is generally included in a person's Will if they have dependent children. This Trust is funded by the terms of the will and goes into effect after the death of the maker of the will. After your death this trust becomes Irrevocable and cannot be changed.

Living Trusts.

Any Trust that takes effect during the Trust Maker's lifetime is considered a Living Trust. Living Trusts are a form of Revocable Trust. The creator of the Trust designates himself or herself as trustee while he or she is alive.

The greatest advantage to having a Living Revocable Trust is that you can buy and sell assets at will. If you want to leave a particular item to a grandchild or child, you just have to make a declaration to who should receive the item. If you have a daughter and a son, you could leave your jewelry to your daughter and all tools to your son.

This type of Trust becomes Irrevocable at the time of your death, meaning that the Trustee will have to disburse your assets to the Beneficiaries without changing any of your wishes. All Control of your assets and money is directly under your control until you die.

Reasons that this is recommended:

A Living Trust can be defunded if or when you become disabled, the alternate Trustee, can manage your assets in the trust.

These trusts can make it easier to manage a disabled heir's inheritance. If a disabled heir was receiving government assistance and would lose that assistance if he or she were to receive an inheritance. The trustee could pay for things for the benefit of the disabled heir, rather than distributing the money to him or her. A properly crafted trust could allow the trustee to buy a house and allow the disabled heir to live there rent-free and pay the bills for the house. The Trustee could buy a car for the use of the heir.

A Revocable Living Trust can be an essential piece of keeping the peace, especially in second or subsequent marriages.

Upon the death of the last Trust Maker, The Revocable Living Trust will become an Irrevocable Trust and nothing can be changed. Everything in the will be distributed to the beneficiaries.

With a Trust, you should also have a Pour- over Will. A Pour– over Will is a mechanism to ensure that anything you did not put in the Trust will go through probate into your Trust.

A Living Trust will be more expensive to set up than a will. The expense is greater now but less work and time and expense for your heirs.

Find an Attorney who specializes in Trusts and Estate Planning or an Elder Law Attorney. This attorney should spend at least Seventy-Five percent of their time practicing in this area of the law.

Differences between a Will and a Trust

Last Will and Testament	Trust
Cheaper to do now	More expensive now
Must go through the Probate Process	No Probate
You can name a guardian for a minor child	Cannot name a guardian for a minor child
Executor to manage assets	Trustee to manage assets
Executor overseen by the court	No oversight by the Court
Public Document	Private Document
Assets are frozen-under the supervision of the court	Assets almost immediately distributed by the Trustee
Creditors can make a claim	Harder for creditors to make a claim
Assets in other states, Probate there	No Probate in other states
Move to another state – New Will must be made in that State.	No changes required
Probate is a longer Process and can take years.	No Probate
Almost anyone can contest a will	Much harder to contest a Trust
More work, time and expense for family	Minimal work, time and expense

9: What is Probate?

Where there is a Will or No Will, There is Probate

Probate refers to the method, by which your estate is administered through the legal system after you die. The probate process helps transfer your estate in an orderly and supervised manner. Probate court is a state court and therefore each state has its own rules.

Because the Probate Court is not a Federal court but a State court, different laws apply in each state.

Probate can be expensive. It is almost impossible to find out what the costs are. Some states have the rate set in law, in other states attorneys, accountants and others can charge whatever they want to.

As soon as your will is submitted to the Probate Court, your will becomes a matter of public record. Anyone can view your will, private financial information and business information.

When you die, the work begins for the Executor of your Will. He or she will become responsible to do all the work that the court asks of them. Your Will is presented to a court officer for filing. This petition actually starts the probate process. Your will determines how your estate will be transferred during the probate process. If a will is in place, the probate court will admit your will acknowledging its validity.

The Executor of your will have the responsibility of carrying out basic steps.

The most basic probate process involves two steps:

- Pay the debts that you owe.

- Transfer assets to your beneficiaries.

Depending on what State you live in, your Executor may be required to:

- Be sworn in as your representative.

- Notify heirs, creditors and the public that you are dead.

- Publish a death notice. This notice makes your estate part of the public record.

- Inventory your property, real and personal. One reason for this is the executor needs to make sure you left enough to cover any outstanding debt. This also allows the executor to make sure everything is present and accounted for.

- Distribute your estate as to your wishes. This includes, paying bills and any taxes.

The court will determine the Personal Representative or Executor for your estate under the following circumstances:

- If you die without a will, have assets and are single and not married.

- You have a Will, but you did not name an Executor.

- The person you had selected has died or for some reason cannot serve and you forgot to name a backup.

- A family member, such as a spouse or adult child can request the court to appoint them as your Personal Representative. The court gives this person the authority to act on the behalf of your estate. This person will receive a certified document called the Letters of Administration.

Your personal representative files a document called a Petition for Probate of Will with the Probate Court. This petition begins the Probate process.

Some States require your representative to issue a Death Notice in your local newspaper. Death Notice serves as a public notice of your estate's probate and enables creditors to file a claim against your estate within a specified time.

Creditors, who have valid claims, are paid in a certain order depending on the State you live in. Usually, your estate administration costs are the first to be paid. Allowances, funeral expenses and taxes, family and all remaining claims usually follow these costs. All remaining assets are distributed to your heirs and beneficiaries. When there is no will in place, or only part of your estate is protected by a will, the laws where you live will decide how your estate is distributed. To avoid any confusion or hard feelings within your family, a will should be created. When you have not properly planned, the probate process can drag on for years.

As soon as your will is submitted to the Probate Court, your will becomes a matter of public record. Anyone can view your will, private financial information and business information.

During the Probate process, it is relatively easy to challenge your will. Any family member and some people not considered family can make a challenge. Most challenges are not successful but they can lead to family fights in public court. Challenges make the settlement process longer, more expensive and add aggravation to everyone involved.

An inheritance often disqualifies the disabled person from government assistance programs. This often leads to consulting an attorney and more expense.

Probate cannot protect an inheritance from creditors. Once the distributions have been made from your estate, the person receiving the inheritance, can have it confiscated and applied to any judgment including

- IRS liens, judgment from creditors or former spouses.

- Once the Judge closes the Probate process it is closed, it is over.

- Ordinarily, creditors are not allowed to make any claims against the estate.

-

Exception to the rule:

Spouse or Partner. Jointly owned property (House, Vacation Home or Condo, CD's, Bank Accounts, Life insurance policies with a defined beneficiary,401k plans or individual retirement accounts(IRA), again with a named beneficiary do not have to go through the probate process.

How to transfer assets to heirs free of probate within weeks or at most months

- Make gifts to people before you die. This can be cash or assets.

- Add a "pay upon death" designation to a bank account.

- Hold your house in joint- tenancy with right of survivorship with your spouse or partner.

- Name the beneficiaries for retirement accounts, life insurance policies.

- Establish a Trust if you have many assets and or a business.

10: What is a Power of Attorney?

Powers of Attorney and Durable Powers of Attorney

A Power of Attorney (POA) is a legal document that gives someone you choose the power to act in your place.

An Ordinary or Nondurable Power of Attorney automatically ends if the person who makes the POA loses mental capacity. This happens if you become incapacitated from physical injury or illness or simply from the effects of aging.

The person for whom this Power of Attorney is created is known as the Grantor. The Grantor can only create a POA when he or she has the requisite mental capacity.

In case you ever become mentally incapacitated, you will need what is known as Durable Powers of Attorney for Healthcare and Finances.

Durable Power of Attorney (DPOA):

A Durable Power of Attorney is a legal document that allows you to name the person you trust to act in your behalf, if you are unable to.

In case you ever become mentally incapacitated, either from dementia, a stroke or an accident, you will need to have a Durable Power of Attorney for medical care and finances. A Durable Power of Attorney simply means that the document stays in effect if you become incapacitated and unable to handle matters on your own or until you die.

DPOA for Healthcare:

A valid Durable Power of Attorney for Healthcare will allow the person you named to make medical decisions for you. That is, a Durable Power of Attorney for healthcare is one type of Healthcare Directive – that is, a document that set out your wishes for healthcare if you are ever too ill or injured to speak for yourself. This trusted person will oversee your medical care and make health care decisions for you. The person you name will be your Agent, Attorney in Fact, Healthcare Proxy, Healthcare Surrogate, or something similar.

Your health care agent will work with doctors and other health care providers to make sure you get the medical care you wish to receive.

When arranging your care, your agent, is legally bound to follow your true treatment preferences to the extent that he or she knows about them.

To make your wishes known and clear you can use a second type of Healthcare Directive, often called a Healthcare Declaration or Living Will, to provide written healthcare instructions to your agent and healthcare providers. To make this easier some states combined a Durable Power of Attorney for Healthcare and Health Care Declaration into a single form commonly called an Advanced Health Care Directive.

You can allow your agent to make only certain decisions for you, but unless you specify what they are, your agent will have comprehensive power.

Your agent will be able to:

Consent or refuse any medical treatments.

Hire and fire medical personnel if you are at home.

Make decisions on the best medical facility for you.

Visit you in the hospital even when others are restricted.

Gain access to your medical records and other personal information.

Get Court authorization, if required, to obtain or withhold medical treatment.

Most of your agent's authority, under a Durable Power of Attorney for Healthcare, will end upon your death. As long as you are able to understand and communicate your own wishes, your agent cannot override what you want. You can change or revoke your healthcare documents at any time, providing you are competent and able to communicate.

If you get a divorce and you named your then spouse as your agent, his or her authority is automatically revoked in most States.

It is wise to name an alternate in this document. In case of divorce or make a new document.

DPOA for Finances:

A Financial Power of Attorney is a Power of Attorney prepare that gives someone the authority to handle financial transactions on your behalf. Some financial powers of attorney are very simple and use the single transactions such as closing a real estate deal. But the power of attorney where discussing here is our answer; it's designed to let someone else manage all of your financial affairs for you if you become in capacity and it's called a durable power of attorney for finances.

With a Durable Power of Attorney for finances, you can give a trusted person as much authority over your finances as you like. The person you choose is called an agent, or attorney in fact (not necessarily an attorney), or a trustee, who takes over custody of all financial matters of the grantor watching retirement accounts and other investments or filing your tax returns. Your agent does not have to be a financial expert but someone you trust completely who has a good dose of common sense. If necessary, your agent can hire professionals to help paying for them out of your assets.

A valid Power of Attorney for Finances, will allow the person you named, to legally take care of important matters for you – for example, managing your investment, paying your bills,– if you are unable to do so yourself. If you become incapacitated, your agent can maintain your financial affairs until you are again able to do so without any need of court involvement. This way, your family's needs continue to be provided for, and the risk of financial loss is reduced. A Durable Power of Attorney ends at your death.

Why do you need separate documents for medical care and finance?

You may wonder why you cannot cover healthcare and finances with one Durable Power of Attorney document. Technically, you can – but it is not a good idea.

Making separate documents will keep life simpler for your agent and others. You may want two different people, one in charge of your finances and one in charge of your medical needs.

Your health care documents may have a lot of personal information that your financial agent does not need to know and vice versa.

If you name a different person for each of these documents, make sure they get along well.

The grantor, who creates the Durable Power of Attorney, can only do so, when he or she has the requisite mental capacity.

Note: In order for a Durable Power of Attorney to be a legal document, it must be signed and dated by you, the agent and a witness or Notary Public. This increases the likelihood of withstanding a challenge.

11: What are Healthcare Directives?

Healthcare Directives may be the most important estate planning documents you ever make; giving your family, clear written directions about your end of life wishes. Having a Healthcare Directive can spare them a lot of anguish. Without your guidance, family members and health care providers can easily become uncertain about treatment decisions. Without your guidance, your family can disagree about the course to follow. Consequences are sometimes cause rifts in families that are never resolved.

Be proactive and get this done, especially if you are ill or have risk factors for stroke, have a serious illness or have cancer. Age is a big component now that we are living a lot longer, not necessarily in good health or without pain.

As of the writing of this book, my mother is almost 99 years old and living in a nursing home. She is not in any pain or unhappy. She has dementia. Sometimes she knows me but not always. Her heart is strong but her mind and body are deteriorating. She has given my brother and me great gifts. She did a Living will at age 70. Now, at ninety-eight years old and not able to speak for herself, due to dementia. She speaks but lives in her mind in the past. We know all her wishes and we will abide by them. She does not want any intervention except comfort care. This is all in a Living Will. I am thankful to have her with us and I am thankful that she chooses to die with dignity. My brother and I also have a Durable Power of Attorney and we are able to handle all her affairs and speak for her. After our dad died, she chose her coffin and prepaid her funeral. My mother and father also made a Family Trust when they were in their sixties. My father died several years ago and all we had to do was file the Trust with the State and the Trust will continue to be in force until my mother dies. I will certainly miss her when the time comes for her to leave us. I will always remember her as vibrant wonderful caring and giving woman.

She is my wonderful Mother. I hope all of you will give your family this wonderful gift.

Advanced Directives.

An Advanced Directive is a combination of a Durable Power of Attorney for Healthcare and a Living Will. This document will allow you to give specific instructions about any aspect of your health care and treatment. If you cannot speak for yourself, your agent for the Durable Power of Attorney, will oversee your care and make decisions for you, specified in your Living Will. If you are competent and able to speak, you can let the medical staff know what you want done and you can change your mind at any time.

Living Will

A Living Will is a healthcare declaration. This is also known as a Medical Directive. You make the decision for what you want to be done for you or not to be done if you are not able to speak for yourself. This document will guide your agent or Medical Proxy to take the steps necessary to fulfill your wishes.

The forms that you fill out allow you to choose what you want to have done for you if you are unconscious and cannot speak for yourself. You may choose any of these types of directives not to prolong life if you have an incurable or irreversible condition that will result in your death within a short period.

If you become unconscious and to a reasonable degree of medical certainty, you will not regain consciousness, it is likely that the risks and burdens of treatment will outweigh the expected benefits.

Life Prolonging Medical Care;

You may want to prolong your life as long as possible within limits of generally accepted healthcare standards. However, you can specify in the Living Will forms that you would like any of the following:

- Transfusions of blood and blood products.

- CPR. If your heart stops do, you want the medical personnel to take measures to bring your heartbeat back.

- Diagnostic tests – MRI, Cat Scans, X-rays etc.

- Dialysis – if your kidneys are not functioning well.

- Administration of drugs.

- Use of a respirator- a machine that breathes for you.

- Surgery.

You can check off yes or no to any of the above on the Living Will Documents or you can check off.

Prolong Life within the limits of generally accepted healthcare standards.

Food and Water;

If you are close to death from a serious illness or are permanently comatose (unconscious), you may not be able to survive without food and water.

Unless you check off NO on the Healthcare Directive, Doctors will use Intravenous (IV) feeding or tubes to provide you with nutrients and fluids. They will do this through an arm or leg vein.

If you choose YES to Food and Water, you could live years in a comatose state.

As long as you are able to communicate your wishes, by whatever means, you will never be denied food or water.

Palliative Care;

If you want death to occur naturally without life prolonging measures taken, it does not mean you cannot receive pain medications. These medications are referred to as comfort care. This is now called Palliative Care.

Palliative Care emphasizes quality of life and dignity. This type of care keeps you comfortable and free of pain until death occurs naturally.

Palliative Care can be administered at home, in a Hospice facility or in a hospital.

You can check off yes on the Living Will form to relieve pain or discomfort even if it hastens your death.

Optional Specifications;

You may also include wishes about donating your organs. You can specify what organs or tissue that you would like to donate if viable. You may give your organs to research. You may also specify the purpose of your donation such as transplant, therapy research or education.

Organ Donation

Every hospital in the USA that receives government funding or Medicare payments has to notify the organ bank when a person dies in the ER.

If your loved one is a candidate, the Organ Bank will call the contact family member. They will do an interview with the contact person. They will ask about all the medical history of the deceased. This can be for an hour or more in some cases. This is very difficult for the person being interviewed and in grief.

Vital organs that can be donated for transplant are; heart, lungs, liver, pancreas, kidney and small intestine.

Tissue grafts that can be donated are; corneas, heart valves, bones ulna and radius (lower arm), humerus (upper arm), Femur (upper leg), Tibia and Fibula (lower leg) and heel (foot), skin, veins, arteries, connective tissue, tendons and ligaments.

Vital organs must have oxygen to keep living; therefore, these organs can be transplanted from a donor who is brain dead. Brain death occurs when a severe injury to the brain happens such as a motor vehicle accident, gunshot to the head or a severe blow to the head, stroke or aneurism. The person cannot breathe on his or her own due to brain injury and are put on artificial life support.

The injury causes swelling to the brain and obstructs blood flow to the brain causing the brain tissue to die and the brain to no longer function. This condition is irreversible.

The vital organs can be kept viable (useable) for a couple of days, if artificial mechanical means are used. Using a ventilator that will give oxygen to these organs. The ventilator will be kept on until surgery can be arranged and performed.

The maximum time between surgery and transplantation varies per organ; once the organ or organs have been removed from the brain dead person, the organs are chilled in a fluid to be kept viable.

Time that these organs are viable for transplantation, if kept chilled in fluid varies:

- Heart and lungs 4 to 6 hours,

- Liver Pancreas is 24 hours,

- Kidneys is 72 hours,

- Corneas is 14 days,

- Bone and Skin is 5 years,

- Heart valves is 10 years,

Medically Brain Dead; Meaning zero brain activity that is legally considered dead.

Many tests are done to assure the person is brain dead.

Making sure there are no brainstem reflexes,

Unresponsive to stimuli (dilation of the pupils in the presence of bright light),

An apnea test is performed and the patient is disconnected from the respirator and has no respiratory movement and other tests as well.

If this person is an organ donor, the respirator will be reconnected.

A person's cause of death determines what organs and tissues can be donated.

If the person had cancer in a vital organ, that organ is not viable for organ donation.

Religious Views.

The majority of Religions support organ donation.

AME & AME Zion, African Methodist Episcopal,

Amish, (Amish will consent to transplantation if they are certain that it is for the health and welfare of the transplant recipient. They would be reluctant to agree to transplantation of an organ if the outcome was considered questionable.)

Assembly of God,

Baha'I, (personal conscience),

Baptist, (personal choice),

Brethren. (charitable act),

Buddhism, (individual conscience),

Roman Catholic, (act of love & charity),

Christian Church, Disciples of Christ, (encourage organ donation),

Church of Christ, (Not a religious problem),

Christian Science, (individual decision),

Episcopal, (encourages organ donation),

Greek Orthodox, (not opposed),

Gypsies, (Opposed to organ donation)

Hinduism, (Individual decision),

Independent Conservative Evangelical, (individual decision),

Islam, (permitted),

Jehovah's Witness, (individual decision),

Judaism, Orthodox, Conservative, Reform and Reconstructionist, (encourage donation),

Lutheran Church, (encourages organ donation),

Mennonite, (individual decision),

Moravian, (individual choice),

Mormon, Church of Jesus Christ of Latter-Day Saints, (encourages organ donation)

Pentecostal, (individual decision),

Presbyterian, (encourages donation),

Seventh-Day Adventist, (encourages donation),

Shinto, (not allowed),

Sikh, (acceptable to donate),

Society of Friends, Quakers, (Individual decision),

Unitarian Universalist, (widely supported for donation),

United Church of Christ, (supportive of organ donation)

United Methodist, (encourages or donation),

Most religions regard organ donation as an act of love and charity.

12: What is a Do Not Resuscitate (DNR) Order?
What is a Do Not Intubate Order (DNI) Order?

A Do Not Resuscitate (DNR) Order is a medical order that a Doctor writes. A DNR order is a document signed by your physician. It instructs healthcare personnel not to perform Cardio Pulmonary Resuscitation (CPR) if you stop breathing or if your heart stops beating.

You choose before an emergency occurs. You decide if you want to have CPR or not. This order only pertains to CPR. It does not affect other treatments such as pain medicine, medicines or nutrition.

A Do Not Intubate (DNI) Order is a medical order written by a Doctor. A DNI instructs healthcare providers not to put you on Life Support equipment. This equipment breathes for you and maintains respiration.

A doctor who writes the orders, does so only after talking about it with you and if possible your family or proxy for healthcare.

A DNR order and a DNI order may be part of a hospice care plan. Hospice care is focused on keeping you comfortable, but not on prolonging your life. If you have cancer or are dying due to other diseases and there is a good probability that you will not

If you already have a DNR and or DNI Order, you can always change your mind and request the order be cancelled, if you can speak. If you choose not to have a DNR order, you are now at full code. Full code means that medical personnel must do everything they can to revive you. If you are of advanced age or dying from a terminal illness, this is not a good choice.

Your doctor writes a DNR and DNI order on your medical chart. He can give you information on how to get a wallet card, bracelet to wear, if anything happens to you in a nonhospital setting.

When and if you are unable to make the decision for CPR, your doctor has a written DNR order on file.

It is wise to carry a DNR and or a DNI Order card in your wallet or wear a bracelet because if you were in an accident or something happens to you and your heart stopped, they would not try to resuscitate you.

Your family cannot override a DNR order you signed.

When Paramedics arrive at a site away from the hospital, they are compelled to perform CPR and other measures that could save your life, no matter what the circumstances.

When you come into the Emergency Room, the Physician has about three minutes to find out about you and determine what course of treatment is to be done. They must get all the following information:

- Your name,

- How old you are,

- The medications you are taking,

- The allergies you have,

- Preexisting illnesses,

- Your Primary care physician,

- Any Specialist you may have,

- Surgeries you have had,

- Your vital signs,

- At the same time as examining your heart, lungs and abdomen, reading your EKG. (Electro Cardiogram), ordering tests and medications. A Doctor must determine whether you are dying from an unknown cause or from an expected disease, like advanced liver cancer.

They have to know if you have a Living Will, Healthcare Proxy and a DNR and or DNI order. If you make the decision to have a DNR and or a DNI Order, this will force your family and the emergency room physician not to try to resuscitate you.

Let your family know if you do not want to be resuscitated or put on life sustaining equipment.

Do not wait until a near death crisis to make decisions and plans. No one comes to the Emergency Room composed and happy. This is an emergency and your family should not be put in a position of making these decisions for you.

A DNR and a DNI order is also usually part of Hospice care. Hospice care is a wonderful service provided when someone is dying of cancer or a disease that is not curable. Hospice care is to keep you comfortable, without pain, as you approach death and allows you to die with dignity... Hospice can also help your loved ones accept the fact that the end is coming.

POLST Order.

In many States DNR orders are being included or replaced by the physician's orders for life-sustaining treatment. This is called a POLST form.

In addition to CPR, POLST forms provide directions to healthcare providers about other life-prolonging treatments such as intubation antibiotic use or feeding tubes. This POLST form is not a complete substitute for all of the above-mentioned forms.

13: What Information is needed to obtain a Death Certificate?

When a person dies, a **Legal Pronouncement of Death form is filled out and signed by a Doctor (MD or DO) or Licensed Nurse (RN) or a Medical Examiner (ME). This document is used to create a Disposition of Death document.**

The Doctor, Nurse, or Medical Examiner signs this form depending on the circumstances. If a person dies in the hospital, the Doctor or Nurse in charge will sign this document. If a person dies under Hospice Care, in a Hospice Facility or at home, the Hospice nurse can sign this Disposition of Death. If a person dies in a Nursing Home, the facility physician will sign the Disposition of Death. If a person dies at home, office, workplace, or anywhere but a hospital, expectedly or unexpectedly, not under Hospice Care, you must call 911. The police and ambulance will be sent to the home, office, workplace or other place. This is considered an unattended death. In other words a death without a Doctor or nurse present is considered unattended.

Depending on the circumstances, the Paramedics will try to revive this person, unless there is a Do Not Resuscitate (DNR) order present signed by a Doctor. If they can get any response at all, they will transport the deceased person to the Hospital Emergency Room and a doctor will continue to try to revive and stabilize this person, put them on life support, and order many tests. If their efforts fail, a doctor or nurse will confirm that death has occurred.

The Medical Examiner is called for any death occurring anywhere including a Medical Facility or Hospital depending on the circumstances. After hearing from the police on the circumstances and medical history of the deceased person, he or she will determine if they come to the house or hospital.

If a 30-year-old person becomes unresponsive at home and the police find no evidence of foul play, the police will investigate the circumstances and the Medical Examiner will come to examine the deceased. He or she will call the Pathologist with his findings and a decision will be made as to whether the deceased will be brought to the morgue to be autopsied. The deceased cannot be moved until the Medical Examiner has completed his investigation.

Once the Disposition of Death is signed, the form is sent to the Funeral Home or Crematorium.

The funeral director will fill in the other needed information after speaking with the family.

The information needed for this form is:

- The full name of the deceased including maiden name if married and if more than one marriage, all married names must be included.

- For example, Mary Jane Blog (maiden name) Doe (first marriage) Pepper (second marriage). This would be Mary Jane Blog Doe Pepper.

- Address; Street and Number, City, State and Zip code.

- Date of Birth.

- Social Security Number.

- Occupation of the deceased even if retired.

- Where the deceased was employed.

- Disposition. Time that death is called and cause of death if known.

- Place of Disposition (where the person died).

- Spouse or Partner's Full Name and Address

- The name, address of the person providing the information.

The funeral Director will then forward this information to the State and a Certified Copy of the Death Certificate will be available at the City Clerk of the town or city where the death occurred. Sometimes the funeral director will get the Death Certificate for You.

This may take a few days.

Not all States require the same information, Please check with the funeral director.

14: What has to be done after a Death?

Do immediately.

- Notify family and friends and ask them to notify others. Please do not use Social Media to do this.

- Notify the funeral home or crematorium and make an appointment for the next day

- Notify the deceased's doctors and cancel appointments.

- Handle the care of dependents and pets.

- Notify the deceased employer, if he or she was employed.

Do within a day or two.

- Arrange for the funeral or cremation and prepare an obituary.

- Search for important documents:

- Prepaid burial or cremation.

- A Will or a Trust.

- A life insurance policy.

- Retirement accounts.

- Request, from the employer, if there is any pay due and if there are any death benefits.

- If the deceased was in the military, contact that office and see if there are

- Any death benefits.

- Notify any religious or fraternal group that the deceased belonged to.

- Notify the Social Security Administration. You may call 800-772-1213.

- Pick up multiple Certified Death Certificates; you may need them for life insurance claims, financial institutions, and social security administration. (Sometimes the funeral director will handle contacting the Social Security Administration).

- Notify Attorney if any.

- Notify Accountant if any.

- Notify banks and other financial institutions.

- Notify credit card companies.

- Notify mortgage companies and lenders.

- Notify insurance companies.

- Notify pension companies

- Notify the Veterans Administration if necessary.

Do in the days after the funeral.

Now is the time that you submit the will to the Probate Court. Gather all the important documents necessary for the filing. Hire an attorney to help you if necessary. Be mindful of attorney fees. Some states have a set fee for attorneys and in other states, the attorneys can charge whatever they like.

If the person that died did not have a will but had assets, he has an estate that has to go through the Probate Court.

15: Your Preparation Checklist

In a binder, file or large envelope place the documents your family will need upon your death. Put these documents in a safe place and inform someone you trust where it is, preferably your executor or trustee. I use page protectors to separate all documents and information. I have my list in one and then my will, trust and mark them so it easy to find the information you need. Etc.

Make a list of the following,

- Attorney,- Name, address and telephone number,

- Accountant,- Name, address and telephone number,

- Executor of your Will, - Name, address and telephone number

- Trustee of your Trust, - Name, address and telephone number,

- Agent for your Medical Power of Attorney, - Name address and telephone number,

- Agent for your Financial Power of Attorney, - Name, address and telephone number,

- Stockbroker, - Name, address and telephone number,

- Bank and Credit Unions,

- Bank Accounts or Credit Unions, - Bank or Credit Union name, address, telephone number, account type (savings, or checking), account number, name or names on the account,

- Debts, - Lender name, description and loan number,

- Credit Cards, - Type of Card (M/C, Visa etc.), issuer, account number, name on the card,

- Debit Cards, - Name of Bank or Credit Union, address, telephone number, PIN number.

- CD – Certificates of Deposit – Name on Certificate, account number,

- Safety Deposit Box, - Name of Bank, address, telephone number, name of the box holder, box number, and location of the key.

- Insurance Policies,

- Life Insurance, - Name of Company, address, telephone number, account name and plan number, name of beneficiaries,

- Retirement and Pension Plans,

- Pension Plans, - Name of Company, address, account number and telephone number.

- 401K and Retirement Plans, - Company Name, address, telephone number, account number and contact information,

- Annuities, - Name of Company, address, telephone number, account name and plan number, name of beneficiaries,

- Other,

- Military Pension,

- Property,

- Property Owned, - Description, location, deed, recording page number, Mortgage Company and telephone number,

- Property Insurance, - Name of Company, account number, Titles,

- Vehicles, - RV's – Motorcycles, etc. Tittle, - Insurance, - description and loan information if they are not owned outright,

Legal Documents,

- Will or Pour-over Will,

- Living Will,

- Trust Documents,

- Living Trust,

- Medical Directive and or Advanced Directives,

- Power of Attorney for Finances,

- Power of Attorney for Medical Needs,

- Other Important Documents to have,

- Birth Certificate,

- Marriage Certificate,

- Divorce Decree,

- Social Security Card,

- Military Discharge papers,

- Veterans Administration Service Record, (VA) information,

- Copy of Medicare Card,

- Copy of Medical Supplemental Insurance Card,

- Doctor's name and telephone number,

- Investment Portfolio,

- Last Available Income Tax Return,

Funeral,

- Funeral Home to contact, address, telephone number,

- Pre- Arranged Funeral contract, Location,

- Cemetery Information, - Name of cemetery, address, Plot in whose name, plot number, section, block, location of the deed, name of the administrator of the cemetery,

- Cremation, - Name of crematorium, pre-arranged contract location, disposition of ashes,

- Funeral Services to be held, - Name of the Church or Funeral home or other facility, location,

- Visitation or calling hours to view your body,

- Pallbearers, - Name of people you would like to accompany your body to the Church,

- Flowers, - yes or no,

- Memorial Donations, - Name of the Charity, address,

- Other, - Lodge or Military Service contact,

- Clergyman, - Name of the person conducting the funeral, what scripture readings you selected, clothing that you want to be buried in,

Biographical Information, -

- HS Attended and graduation date
- College Attended and graduation date
- Place of Employment
- Position held
- Retirement date, etc.
- Mother and Fathers' names and date of birth
- Children's names, Location and if they were adopted
- Fraternal Organization Memberships
- Professional Associations
- Church Affiliations
- Political Positions held
- Boards served on
- Special Recognitions

Computer:

- Master Password: password for your computer, tablet, phone, etc.
- E-Mail accounts: Name of account…, User name…, Password…
- All of the following accounts:
- Name…, user name…, password…

- Social Media

- Facebook

- Twitter

- LinkedIn

- Pinterest

- Others

- Others:

- Amazon. Com

- E-Bay.com

- You tube.com

- PayPal.com

- Websites you own:

- Website; acdef.com

- Hosting company

- Domain name

- Programs that you use:

- Wordpress.org

- Microsoft Office

- Security Software

- Others:

- On-Line Banking;

- A list of all the bills that you pay on line

- Automatic withdrawals from your checking account

Appendix A: "IT'S OK TO DIE"

Monica Williams-Murphy, MD & Kristian Murphy

With the permission of Dr. Monica Williams-Murphy, MD, author of the book, "It's OK to die", the following articles and blog posts are recreated here.

Dr. Monica Williams-Murphy, MD, is a board-certified Emergency Physician, a blogger and a public speaker. She works in one of the busiest ER's in the country.

I would like to take this opportunity to thank Dr. Monica Williams-Murphy for inspiring me. Thank you for all you do for others.

You can order her book "It's Okay to Die" on Amazon .com.

Please visit her website: http://www.oktodie.com/blog

Be Careful How You Leave: Creating Peace for All Parties

Tuesday, 13 November 2012

I pulled the stifling surgical mask off my face as I left my last patient's room. I had just finished suturing a complicated facial laceration and was bone-tired from the evening. Glancing at the clock, I saw that mercifully, my shift was over.

Collapsing into my chair to finish my charting, I was slightly annoyed when my nurse held a clipboard in front of my face, "Here is your next patient."

"No, really, I'm done…" I started to explain to her until I saw what was written on the papers held by the clipboard… "Patient is ready to quit dialysis. Son doesn't want him to."

"Oh, I said slipping down deeply into my chair, "I guess this is my patient."
So, taking a deep breath to shake off some of my fatigue, I headed toward
this patient's room. Glancing at the chart before I opened the door, I noted
that the patient's name was Mr. Bryan.

"Knock, Knock…Mr. Bryan?" I called out while pushing the door with my
shoulder.

"That's me," a tired figure said from the hospital bed.

Mr. Bryan was a large framed man of about 70. His physical largeness
accentuated his posture-head hung low almost as if in defeat; shoulders
drooping…tired. His weariness was so profound that my own fatigue
seemed to slip away in insignificance.

I stood up straighter and offered my hand to both Mr. Bryan "senior" and
Mr. Bryan "junior" who sat beside him, "Doctor Murphy, so nice to meet
both of you."

I pulled up a stool next to the elder Mr. Bryan's bed. "My nurse tells me
that, as a family, you are struggling to make decisions about whether to
continue dialysis or not," I stated rather matter-of-factly, not needing to act
as if I did not know the crux of the issue at hand.

My patient, with his head still hanging low, nevertheless raised his eyebrows
with; I think surprise that I was willing to start at the heart of the issue.

Taking my lead, Mr. Bryan unmasked himself and began at the very core of
his own deeply personal saga. What ensued was a conversation unlike any
that I have ever had with a patient before.

"Doctor, I know you are busy, but I have something very complicated to
explain to you. You see, I am a bit of a philosopher, and have done a lot of
reading. I think this whole life thing is some sort of mental construct…and,
when you die, you become free of all of this. Free and unattached from
whatever your life has been, unattached from any of the tragedy of life,
unattached from the entanglements of relationships gone bad or even
good."

I leaned in toward Mr. Bryan to give him my full attention.

He continued, "I just don't think any of this matters after you die…I have come to the point where the physical tax of continuing to live artificially (via 3 times weekly dialysis) has exceeded my desire to stay in this life, and to stay in all of these attachments. I'm ready to be done, to be free."

After a pause, Mr. Bryan said, "My son here will not like hearing me say these things." He looked down at his own white-knuckled grip on the blanket rather than at his son who sat along the opposite bedside.

Mr. Bryan "junior" then explained to me that he was actually "OK" with his father being "done" but that he had asked his father to please continue dialysis until his only sibling, a younger brother could drive down from New England to 'say goodbye" and to have closure. "Surely Doctor, this cannot be too much to ask," he pleaded his case to me.

Mr. Bryan "senior" responded and stated carefully, "But, these relationships won't even matter to me after I'm dead. You and your brother won't have to worry about me after I have left this world."

Finally, I interrupted and said, "But, Sir, you must be careful how you leave."

Mr. Bryan "senior" turned to look me in the eyes for the first time, "What do you mean, Doctor?" and Mr. Bryan "junior" looked toward me with faint hope and surprise.

I had sat very quietly listening without judgment during the preceding conversation. I could understand my patient's perspective, as well as his son's. Both wanted closure, just different types.

However, it suddenly became clear to me that the son's desires should trump my patient's desires. I recognized this as one of the few instances in which I thought the needs of the one dying should be secondary to the needs of others.

I explained to my patient, "Mr. Bryan, in your view, you are 'checking out,' which is fine, you are ready to move on, you have lived a full life… I get it. However, I urge you to think of those of us who you will be leaving behind in this "construct." You will be gone, but your sons will have to go on living. They will still be here entangled together in this thing called life. The manner of your leaving creates a pattern for those left behind, like the cloud trails of a jet plane. If you actually choose to "leave" before your sons have the opportunity to create closure and peace with you, then you are choosing to leave behind a legacy of sorrow and maybe even suffering. In contrast, if you stay a little bit longer, long enough to heal old wounds, and finalize peace, you will leave trails of gratitude. You may be leaving this world, but how you go leaves a lasting impression-an impression which could affect not only your sons, but possibly an entire generation of your family, and others."

Then we all sat quietly looking at each other, and around the room in thought.

I guess my ideas had some merit in my patient's eyes. Mr. Bryan "senior" chose to continue dialysis until his youngest son arrived. I advised expressions of forgiveness and to share the words: "Thank you, I love you and goodbye." I think they took my advice.

In the end, Mr. Bryan and his son crystalized this lesson for us: If we are fortunate enough to die consciously, then we should take full advantage of opportunities to create peace for all parties. Our last words and intentions matter so much to those left behind. We should be careful how we leave.

After note: I am grateful to my nurse who asked me to see this last patient before I left.

(As always, names and some facts have been changed to protect the privacy of the patient.)

Appendix B:

Victims, Inc,

The Joan Ellis Victims Assistance Network

I am very proud to be part of this wonderful organization.

Victims Inc. was created in the memory of Joan Ellis over 20 years ago. Victim's Inc. is a non-profit organization. Victims, Inc. receives a Federal Victims of Crime Act Grant administered by the State Attorney General Office, donations from Corporations, Trusts, Churches and individuals, holiday yard sales and Saturday night Bingo.

Joan and her unborn daughter were killed and her 2-year-old daughter was seriously injured in a motor vehicle crash, caused by a driver who failed to stop at a red light. The devastation caused by the death of this vibrant young woman, led her husband to create a service for victims that did not already exist. Victims, Inc. provides immediate service with trained trauma volunteers prepared to be with people in the worst moments of their lives; volunteers who stay with the families until the family support system is in place.

The Victims Inc. mission is to complete the circle of services for victims from the onset of trauma through healing.

Victims, Inc. trains Trauma Intervention Volunteers to be on call 24 hours a day to assist victims and families in two counties in our State of New Hampshire.

Trauma Intervention Volunteers respond to pages from Police, Fire and Emergency Medical Personnel. They meet families at hospitals, at scenes and in their homes. They respond to serious injury and fatal crashes, fires, robberies, missing persons, suicides, drowning and other premature deaths. They offer comfort, compassion, information and referrals.

Victims, Inc. provides the following services:

To arrive on the scene and free the first responders to continue the work that they are trained to do.

Assist police in doing death notifications.

Follow up on every trauma call.

Work with law enforcement, courts, schools, fire, emergency medical personnel, media, clergy and other non- profit agencies, training volunteers and responding to needs.

To reach out to families after the initial days of the tragedy with sympathy cards, laminated obituaries, and crocheted snowflakes at Christmas and holiday and anniversary cards. Victims, Inc. provides gifts each December for all of the children served by our program during the year.

Contacts and offers services to victims of all fatal crashes in NH.

To attend motor vehicle hearings with surviving family members of people killed in crashes.

To accompany people through the court process as they attend hearings, trials, sentencing, parole and other legal proceedings.

To assist victims in filing applications for state funded victim's compensation.

To notifies victims of pertinent legislative hearings and accompanies them to hearings.

Resource Page

Nolo.com/legal

Eldercareteam.com/public

Williamsburgmemorialpark.com

Macmillan.org/endoflife.UK

caringinfo.org

Dummies.com

About.com

EHow.com

LegalForms.LawDepot.com

Nlm.nih.gov/MedlinePlus

Rocketlawyer.com

Wikipedia.org

Living trust

Essortment.com

Ontheweb.com

HospiceFoundation.org

NAELA.org   National Academy of Elder Law Attorneys

Books;

"It's OK to Die" by Monica Williams Murphy, MD, and Kristian Murphy.

"I Wasn't Ready to Say Goodbye" by Brook Noel and Pamela D. Blair, PhD.

"Surviving, Coping & Healing after the Death of a Loved One."

"How to go on Living when someone you Love Dies" by Therese A. Rand, PhD.

"Helping you get through Grief".

ABOUT THE AUTHOR

My name is Marie Robinson. I was born and brought up in New Hampshire, where I still reside. I am married to a wonderful man, who was my high school sweetheart. We have two beautiful children and two grandchildren.

I have been in the medical field as an X-Ray Technologist, an entrepreneur in business as a VP of a Corporation handling all the finances, a mom and a memere. (Grandmother in French).

I have had a wonderful life and have been fortunate to live my passion twice.

A few years ago, after I retired from the Medical Field, my daughter-in-law brought in an ad for training to become a Trauma Intervention Volunteer. I did the training and became a Trauma Intervention Volunteer for Victims, Inc. Here is where I found my second passion, helping and assisting people and families at the worst time of their lives. Losing a loved one to death is very difficult. I know I make a difference most of the time and that is rewarding to me. That brings us to why I have written this book. In my experience as a Trauma Intervention Volunteer, I have seen many tragedies and families have become estranged because of the lack of planning for the end of life; making decisions that are hard to make and where not all involved agree.

I want you to be aware of all that is available to you so that you will not leave your loved ones in a big mess to deal with upon your death.

I would like to end by saying, "Send Me the Flowers before You Die".

Thank you so much for reading this book. I hope you have gained insights into this important topic.

Share the knowledge you have learned and help others from the horror stories I have shared with you.

Start the conversation with parents, adult children and friends.

Get to know me:

Marie C.Robinson

E-Mail; MeetMarieRobinson@gmail.com

Blog: <http://meetmarierobinson.com/>

Twitter: http://MarieCRobinson

Linkedin: http://MarieRobinson

Facebook http://Facebook.com/Marie Carrier Robinson

One Last Thing:

If you enjoyed this book or found it useful, I would be very grateful if you would post a short honest review on Amazon.com. Your support really does make a difference and I read all the reviews personally so I can get your feedback and make this book even better.

If you would like to leave a review then all you need to do is click the review link on this books' page on Amazon.com.

http://www.amazon.com/dp/B011Z5R1VY

Thank you for again for your support!

Wishing you peace and happiness.

Marie C. Robinson

Made in the USA
Middletown, DE
20 October 2015